PURSUING A DREAM TO FLY

Bob Murray

Writers Club Press

San Jose New York Lincoln Shanghai

Pursuing a Dream to Fly

Writers Club Press
an imprint of iUniverse.com, Inc.

For information address:
iUniverse.com, Inc.
620 North 48th Street
Suite 201
Lincoln, NE 68504-3467
www.iuniverse.com

ISBN: 0-595-12217-5

Printed in the United States of America

This book is dedicated to my father,
the late George Edward Murray (1918-1996).
Thank you for giving me the ability to succeed
and the ambition to pursue a dream.

CONTENTS

Acknowledgements

My sincerest gratitude to the office staff and instructors at Commercial Aviation Corporation. Al Beckwith and his staff provided quality services, well maintained equipment and expert instruction. It was a pleasure to fly with professional and patient instructors like Jim Masterson, Bill Bryant, Mike Anthony and Herb McGaughey. Thanks to Becky Scaglione for cheerfully handling my account.

Bill Bradshaw, my pilot friend, unknowingly provided the spark that got me started down the path of learning to fly and I am deeply grateful.

Special thanks to Charlotte Murray, Nancy Randall, Janet McKee, Bill Lohan and Fred Bishop for your candid feedback and encouragement in the development of this book.

INTRODUCTION

My father, George Edward Murray, gave me some advice shortly before his death in 1996 at the age of 78. He said, "If there is something you really want to do, do it! Don't wait until you're too old to do it or enjoy it, whatever it may be. Just do it!"

I know there were things Dad wanted to do in his lifetime, but he grew too old and unhealthy to pursue them. It saddened me to see him physically deteriorate, knowing that his heart and mind were ready and willing to travel, fish, and otherwise enjoy his well-deserved retirement. But he couldn't. Sure, he had the money, but as he said once, "What good is money if you can't do what you really want to do?"

Shortly after I graduated from high school in 1973, I had the opportunity to take a plane trip with a friend and his father in a small four-seat airplane. I loved it! I was in awe as I watched ground drop away as we lifted off. Suddenly the drab corn and soybean fields of southern Illinois turned into an incredibly beautiful patchwork mosaic. Watching his dad control a beautiful piece of machinery that could actually take off, dive and soar in the sky ignited a spark of desire within my soul to learn to fly as well!

Then life took over. Time went by. I started then finished college, got married and started my family and career. The thoughts of that first flight gradually faded into the background. But the spark of desire kindled that day was still alive and burning in my heart. Several years later, at the age of 42, it reasserted itself. But by then I had a family to support and a career to manage like everyone else. There just wasn't enough time to pursue my dream of learning to fly. My father's words, however, about not waiting too long to pursue a dream, also echoed in my mind.

In the summer of 1997 I met a pilot at a neighborhood party. As the evening progressed, Bill and I talked for several hours about flying; what skills and preparation are required, and how to start the learning process. As we talked, the flame of desire that was sparked on that first flight as a teenager began smoldering. Before we parted that evening, Bill asked if I would like to fly with him sometime and I accepted his invitation. As it turned out, he called the next weekend and asked if my twelve-year-old son, Greg and I would like to go for a short flight in his airplane. There was no way we were going to turn that down!

We met Bill at his home and drove to the airport. The short flight that afternoon, and the impact of my father's advice years earlier, fully ignited the dream that had been smoldering in my heart! I knew what I needed to do.

For the next two months I considered the time and effort it would take to learn to fly an airplane, bought several books on the subject, and talked with others who had started to learn, but had stopped short of realizing their goal. I developed a keen interest in flying and could not get enough information on the subject. At the end of those two months, I finally decided that there was no time like the present to pursue this goal. It was now or never. I called several airports in the local area to get information about flight training available and each invited me to take an introductory flight with their trainers. In mid-September of 1997 I scheduled an appointment with Commercial Aviation at the Kent State University Airport in Stow, Ohio. They were as qualified as the others I talked to, but I chose them mostly for convenience. The airport and training facility was only a five-minute drive from my home.

In spite of all the reading and investigation I undertook about learning to fly, I never really knew what to expect from the entire learning process. If you, the reader, are pursuing a dream to fly, I hope this narrative of my experiences will assist you to understand the process and what could be in store for you. If you are already a licensed pilot I hope my story brings back pleasant memories.

To me, learning to fly an airplane was like growing up. I went from a virtually helpless infant to a graduate in less than a year. I had my father's advice and the wisdom he passed on, the love and support of my wife and family, and forty-two years of life lessons. I was armed with logic, confidence, perseverance, ability, desire and common sense. I was also saddled with fear, anxiety, doubt, responsibility and a wild imagination! Each of these would play a role in my development.

What follows is the chronology of my flight training from the introductory flight through Private Pilot certification. Like most journeys into the unknown, it was an amazing one with unexpected twists and turns. It was challenging, stimulating, frustrating, humbling and enjoyable. I've also learned that it never ends. I learn something new every time I fly. Kind of like life.

GETTING STARTED

Starting flight training is like starting a new job. It's a strange environment with new faces and places, terminology and rituals. As a new student, I haven't earned any respect, I'm unsure of what to do and I'm self conscious about my lack of knowledge and skill. I am, however, confident that, eventually, I'll get used to it and I'm confident that I can succeed.

I know only what I've read about why an airplane flies and the controls needed. I know virtually nothing about weather, instruments, where to look, when to react, what's normal and what's not. In this environment, I'm quite insecure, unlike most of the rest of my life which is quite comfortable and familiar. My goal is to learn everything I can about flying. I not only want to be a pilot, but I want to be a great pilot.

Saturday, September 20, 1997 Total Hours: 0

On a gloomy Saturday morning, I went to the Kent State University airport for an introductory flight. Kent State operates a small non-towered airport with one asphalt runway.

Non-towered means that there is no controller sitting in a control tower carefully orchestrating the arrival and departure of aircraft. Non-towered is sometimes called uncontrolled. If everyone plays by the rules, however, there is some semblance of control.

The runway runs north (number 01) and south (number 19). It's 4000 feet long and as wide as five lanes of traffic. It sounds big but it looks very small from the air. Most large airport runways are two to three times as wide and sometimes two to three times as long.

Runways are numbered according to their magnetic direction minus the last zero. For example, a runway pointing east or 090 degrees from north is numbered 09. The opposite end of the runway is numbered 27 since it points west or 270 degrees from north.

The weather was rainy and overcast, something I would have to get used to. I never really paid attention to the weather before, but I would learn that a large part of flying is knowing about weather conditions.

I met Jim, my Certified Flight Instructor (CFI). He's a young guy, not long out of college with aspirations to be a charter pilot or corporate pilot. He's also been an instructor for about six months. I soon found out that being a flight instructor is a career step toward the ultimate airline position. Flight instructors can log time watching students sweat in the air. Flight time is one of the entry criteria for flying the big commercial airplanes. It isn't surprising that a young flight instructor can pass through the flight instructor stage and move on faster than a slow student like me can learn to fly. I guess that it is rare to start and finish flight training with the same instructor who is also climbing the career ladder.

After watching an introductory video and reviewing the new student kit, Jim and I went to pick out an airplane. Behind each hangar door was an airplane with different characteristics and prices. Jim explained the advantages of each of seven available Cessna's with the enthusiasm of a used car salesman. It was obvious that he enjoyed being around airplanes.

We sat in most of them to get a feel for how much room they provide. It looks like the Cessna 172 is probably the best choice because it has four seats and I'll probably want that later. With both of us sitting in the airplane, the 172 had more elbow room than the 152. Not much more, but some. Also, it's in my price range.

We then reviewed the expected costs, insurance, and the requirements for being a pilot. The Federal Aviation Administration (FAA) is very specific about the requirements for a private pilot. There are clear expectations that include the experience required, the minimum amount of training, the written test requirements and the practical test standards. I found it helpful to know what was expected of me because it helped me put my training in perspective and I could usually determine why my instructor was drilling me on maneuvers and knowledge.

Even at this early stage, I began to learn three basic lessons. First, flying skills are only a part of the total package of being a pilot in today's airspace. There are other details like weather knowledge, navigation skills, planning, aircraft requirements, communications, pilot requirements, emergencies, judgment and many more things that just as important.

Second, the making of a good pilot takes years of incremental building of knowledge and skills. Obtaining the license is just the beginning. It's like getting a college degree. It gets you in the door but the real learning takes place in the real world. You have to recognize your limits and use sound judgment to safely stretch beyond your comfort zone without taking too much risk. Fortunately, as a student pilot, you have your instructor to guide you.

Third, the regulations often state legal minimums. For example, as a visual flight rule (VFR) pilot, you can't legally fly with less than three miles of visibility. It sounds like a lot, but without considerable experience, three miles is not enough for the novice navigator. You can legally fly with a one thousand foot overcast but you have to be five hundred feet below the clouds. That means that it is legal to blaze along at five hundred feet above the ground but you have to watch out for towers and other obstructions. What will you do if the ceiling drops a few hundred feet? Under what conditions would you expect the overcast to descend to the earth?

Because of the rain, we rescheduled the introductory flight for Sunday at 10:00 A.M., weather permitting. I then met Al, the owner of the company. He asked about my desire to learn to fly and told me a bit about the requirements. He also reassured me that his is a quality operation that may cost a little more, but will be worth it. Overall I had a satisfactory impression with the people, equipment and company.

Sunday, September 21, 1997 Total Hours: 0.5

Airplanes are referred to by their tail numbers, the numbers and letters painted on the tail of the aircraft. Tail numbers are assigned by the FAA when the airplane is registered. There is a commonly used phonetic alphabet that I'll need to learn. For example, A is alpha, B is bravo, Y is yankee, W is whiskey, and so on. Aircraft are often referenced by the last three positions of the tail number. For instance, tail number N2497Y is commonly called niner-seven-yankee. 'Niner' is used in place of nine so as not to be confused with the German 'nein' which means no.

The airplane I'll normally fly is N2497Y, a 1963 Cessna 172D. It was in for maintenance so we took N54064, a 1981 Cessna 172. Jim did the preflight check as I watched in awe.

Jim let me taxi on the straight parts and he taxied around the turns. After driving a car for several years, I found steering with my feet very awkward. Jim constantly reminded me that turning the yoke (that suspiciously looks like a steering wheel) while on the ground does not make the airplane turn. He threatened to make me sit on my hands to force me to steer with my feet. Using the brakes to stop was also awkward because there are two of them, one for each main wheel.

I followed the written checklist in preparation for takeoff. Checklists are important tools used to verify that all the important items are reviewed before, during and after flight. I found those in the owner's manual to be too basic, so I made my own. After several revisions, I designed one that I liked and I used often. Each airplane is different and requires the checklist to be customized for the different design characteristics, instruments, radios, flying speeds and emergency procedures.

We departed to the north using runway 01 and we had a smooth flight up to the Ohio Turnpike then turned to the west. We did a couple of turns at about 3000 feet MSL (mean sea level). I turned the yoke, to control the ailerons.

The ailerons are located on the trailing edge of each wing near its tip. When the yoke is turned left, the left aileron goes up and the right aileron goes down. This changes the shape of the wing creating more lift on the right side and less lift on the left. This causes the airplane to bank.

Jim controlled the rudder, a vertical flap attached to the tail controlled by the foot pedals. The rudder keeps the tail following directly behind the nose of the airplane resulting in efficient and coordinated flight.

Like they say, time flies when you're having fun. In no time we were landing back at Kent. I was hooked!

Following the flight, we put the airplane in the hangar. Total time .5 hours. I paid $50 for the introductory ride and $300 for share/lease for the year. Share/lease allows me to pay some of the costs up front and then rent an airplane at a lower fee.

I scheduled three more sessions. I am very eager to be able to fly for a whole hour. Next Wednesday is a ground lesson and the next flight is scheduled for September 30.

Wednesday, September 24, 1997 Total Hours: 0.5

I met with Jim at 6:30 P.M. to begin ground lessons.

There are many things that a pilot needs to know that are best learned on the ground. Regulations, weather, aircraft systems, fundamentals of flight, communications and other items are best discussed before getting into the air. It's hard to assimilate new information when you have a white knuckled grip on the yoke during a power-off stall! One of the objectives for ground school is to prepare the student for the written and oral exams but, the primary reason is to prepare the pilot for safe and knowledgeable flight.

A student pilot has several options for ground lessons. They include formal classroom training, individualized training from a CFI, and home study. In a formal program, the student attends regularly schedule training classes with several other students led by a certified ground instructor who has been trained in aviation and fundamentals of instruction. In my area, I am not aware of any such classes outside of the local university. It's interesting to note that a certified ground instructor doesn't have to be a pilot but most of them are.

Another option is to get individualized ground instruction from a CFI. Part of the requirement of obtaining the certified flight instructor rating is to also pass the fundamentals of instruction test. Any CFI then, is qualified to teach ground school.

A final option is home study. There is a wealth of information available for the student to obtain on his own. The Federal Aviation Regulations/Aeronautical Information Manual (FAR/AIM) is updated annually and describes the regulations and generally accepted practices in aviation. Many textbooks are available as well as magazines and videos. The Internet is loaded with aviation links. I found the Internet newsgroup *rec.aviation.student* to be very interesting. It's good to get several explanations from various sources to really understand a concept. The challenge with home study, however, is to stay synchronized with your flight training. It's tempting to skip over the basics to get to the good stuff. Resist this temptation! Fundamentals must be thoroughly understood in order for the rest to make sense.

My ground training was a combination of the latter two options with most of my learning coming from self study. All of my instructors were very knowledgeable but their strengths were in flight training, not ground training. We followed a syllabus for flight training that also identified reading assignments and ground lessons. It was left up to me to keep up with the reading.

Sometimes our discussions about ground training were like a parent talking to their child about sex. It went something like this:

"How are you doing with your study of airspace?"

"Fine."

"OK, well, if you have any questions, just ask. Let's go fly!"

I picked up the student kit and headset that had been ordered for me. The student kit included the textbook, a workbook, the syllabus, a couple of sample maps and an E6B 'whiz wheel' calculator. The E6B looks like a round slide rule, if you know what a slide rule looks like. It can be used to calculate wind correction angles, time, distance, fuel consumption and other useful things. Frankly, I learned enough to know what it did and never used it again. I bought a special aviation calculator instead. I know, the E6B would never run low on batteries, but its a risk I'm willing to take. We reviewed the contents of the kit and I watched the first video on preflight, taxiing, turns, climbs, descents and traffic patterns. Videos are an excellent way to learn about flying. While not getting the feel of what is happening, you can get the visual aspect of it and hear the thought process of an experienced pilot during the particular phase of training.

Next, we went out to the hangar to look at N2497Y while the engine cover, called the cowling, was off and we could see the engine. Jim pointed out the major components of the engine and controls and I had some questions answered about the instruments.

Jim gave me some assignments to read in the textbooks. He also asked me to study the symbols on the sectional (an aeronautical map) and read the airplane owner's manual. The owner's manual for this airplane is a thin, flimsy, little booklet that describes the airplane, normal procedures, limitations and emergency procedures. Toasters come with more documentation! I scheduled a flight lesson for next Tuesday.

Tuesday, September 30, 1997 Total Hours: 0.5

High wind, low clouds and rain meant no flight today. I rescheduled for tomorrow and met with Jim for an hour. We went over weather information. He told me how to set up my home computer to get the Direct User Access Terminal System (DUATS) weather information. This proved to be one of the handiest tools and it didn't cost anything. I downloaded the software from the Internet and have used it since. We used the computer and reviewed the weather data. Jim also explained airspace to me.

The FAA has classified the airspace above the earth's surface. It's either controlled by Air Traffic Control (ATC) or uncontrolled. Major airports are located in Class B airspace which has more rules and restrictions than smaller, less congested airports. I found this to be very confusing, but each type of airspace is clearly marked on the sectional map and, after a while, it gets easier to understand.

This is important because the sky is alive with heavy, fast aircraft around a major airport. A light, general aviation aircraft like a Cessna is no match for a 737. In fact, I've read where just the jet blast of a taxiing airliner was enough to flip a Cessna upside down on the taxi way. An airliner in flight generates an invisible tornado off its wing tips that can literally turn a light aircraft upside down in the air!

I took the 'advanced maneuvers' video home with me. The rest of my new student kit came in including the Practical Test Standard (PTS), a plotter and the Federal Aviation Regulations (FAR).

The PTS is a small booklet that clearly explains the required knowledge and skills that must be demonstrated during the practical test (the oral and checkride). It also defines the standards of performance that must be met.

Weather looks good for flying tomorrow. I'm pretty anxious.

I can't wait to really get started. I've studied books, workbooks, charts, videos and other tools of the piloting trade. At this stage, I have the impression that this is going to be easy. After all, the FAA says you only need 20 hours of instruction and 40 total hours of experience. I expect it's going to be like learning to drive.

My 16 year old daughter, Melissa, will learn to drive soon and I've thought quite a lot about how she will learn. I expect that learning to fly is much the same. I'm very comfortable behind the wheel of a car and I look forward to the same comfort level while flying.

BASIC TRAINING

I'm at the infant stage of my development. Everything I do is under the careful scrutiny of my instructor. I don't know enough to know where to start.

Realistically, I think flying is dangerous, but I don't really know why. I don't know enough to know what to fear. Living near the airport, I can sit on my deck and watch airplanes buzzing around all the time and I don't hear about any crashes. It must not be too dangerous.

Throughout my life, I've tended to want to hurry through the fundamentals to get to the really fun or challenging parts. Dad did teach me a little common sense, however. I realized that there is an element of danger and resolved to really master the basics. I wanted to get over the feeling of being a 'newbie'. With these feelings and thoughts, I started on the journey.

Wednesday, October 1, 1997 Total Hours: 1.5

Finally, my first real lesson. Jim let me do most of the preflight by following the checklists. I started the airplane and taxied out to the runup spot for runway 01. The runup spot is a place near the end of the runway where pilots rev up the engine to ensure that it is working properly. I still don't quite have the feel for taxiing, but I'm getting better. I think I controlled the speed OK.

I followed instructions and felt like I did most of the takeoff up to about 3000 feet MSL. We continued north and I learned to trim the airplane, did some medium bank turns left and right, one 360 degree turn, a climb and level off, and descent and level off. The trim control is a small wheel that is turned to relieve forward or backward pressure that is being applied to the yoke. We cruised at 100-110 mph. We approached the Portage County airport from the north, circled around and entered the traffic pattern for runway 27.

The traffic pattern is a rectangle around the runway. On the downwind leg you fly parallel to the runway in the direction of the wind. On the base leg, you turn left (at most airports) toward the runway and on the final leg you turn left again and line up with the runway. You always try to land into the wind.

I lightly touched the controls and felt what Jim did as he made the landing at about 75 mph. I can tell that this is a difficult part of flying and it will take a lot of practice to master it. There is a lot going on during the approach and touchdown.

After landing, Jim instructed me to taxi back to the end of runway 27 and we took off again into the sun. There was a slight crosswind from the north so we held ailerons into the wind. At 2700 feet we cruised west and then circled back to approach left downwind of runway 01 at Kent. Jim instructed me to radio to get runway information. I picked up the microphone hanging on the side of the cockpit and he said, "Just push the button on the yoke, that's why we have headsets!" I really wanted to use that cool little microphone. I followed Jim through the landing, taxied to the fuel station for a top off, taxied to the hangar and put the airplane inside.

There is almost as much skill required to put the airplane in the hangar as there is to fly the darn thing! You attach a tow bar to the front wheel and push it backwards, steering with the tow bar. The object is to get the airplane in straight without crunching a wing on the side of the hangar door.

That was a fast hour and I was pretty tense the whole way. Can't wait to go again! We scheduled about 8 more lessons through the end of October. For this trip we used about 10 gallons of aviation fuel and the

Hobbs (a meter similar to that in a taxi cab) read exactly one hour. Next flight is 8:00 A.M. Friday if I can get off work.

Friday, October 3, 1997 Total Hours: 2.4

I negotiated with my boss to take vacation time in two hour increments. At 8:00 A.M. I did the preflight with much more confidence and speed. I started the engine and taxied out to the runup spot after radioing to get a radio check and airport advisory.

Technically, at a non-towered airport, a pilot can use whatever runway he chooses. Someone in the airport office will provide an airport advisory based on the direction and strength of the wind and the runway that other pilots have used. It's safer to take off and land into the wind and the active runway can change if there is a shift in its direction. There are windsocks located near the runway to help pilots make the safest choice.

I did the takeoff from runway 19 with little assistance and headed northeast. On the way, Jim expressed some amazement at the tailwind that pushed us along. The airspeed indicator said 90 mph (78 knots per hour) and the LORAN (LOng RAnge Navigation radio) said our ground speed was 140 knots. I did climbs and descents, turns, and remembered to use a little more rudder this time to keep the nose of the airplane pointed straight ahead. We also did some work on the effects of the flaps and changing the airplane configuration.

Flaps are attached to the trailing edge of each wing, near the body of the airplane. In this airplane, they are controlled by a mechanical lever located on the floor of the cockpit, between the seats that lowers the flaps in 10 degree increments. (It looks like an emergency brake handle of a car.) This increases drag and lets you fly slower. The more flaps you put in, the slower you can fly. You can actually fly as slow as 40 mph This is very helpful when you are about to land.

We performed a couple of 360 degree turns, one at 30 degrees of bank and one at 45 degrees (mostly Jim), then headed back. The tailwind turned into a headwind and it took forever to get back. The airspeed indicator said 100 mph (87 knots per hour) and the LORAN said our ground speed was 40 knots! I looked down at the ground and it appeared that we were barely moving.

I entered downwind for runway 19 from a 45 degree angle (brown water tank in the woods near the city of Kent) and Jim talked me through the landing while he did nearly all of it. We pulled up to the fuel station and got out.

At the fuel pump, the line crew came out and put fuel in each of the wings. If you ask, they'll wash the windshield. Then they hook up a tow bar and tow the airplane to the hangar using a small tractor.

Off to work. I felt a whole lot more comfortable today with taxiing, speed control, climbs and using the flaps. I think I'm starting to get used to the airplane. Jim told me I did great so I felt very good about the lesson. He said he likes to start teaching landings after about 5 hours. I guess I'm halfway there.

Sunday, October 5, 1997 Total Hours: 3.4

Awesome! It was very foggy at 9:00 A.M., and my lesson was scheduled for 10:00 A.M. The weather report said it was clear above the fog. By the time I got to the airport the fog had lifted.

I preflighted, taxied and did the takeoff from runway 19 with very little assistance. We flew east where the front line was for the very low clouds. It was awesome! I did some turns in slow flight.

In slow flight the airplane is flown at the slowest possible speed without falling out of the sky. When a plane begins to fall out of the sky, it's called a stall. If the stall goes on too long, it's called a spin. If the spin goes on too long, it's called a crash!

The purpose of the slow flight maneuver is to practice simulated landing conditions at a safe altitude. When landing, the plane is flown very slowly just inches from the runway. About 5 to 10 miles per hour before stall, a cockpit buzzer emits a sick, high pitched, whining sound as a warning. This is generally not good unless you are purposefully flying slow.

I practiced setting up for landing by adding flaps, maintaining the proper speed and controlling the descent rate. We did this a couple of times from 3000 feet down to about 1500 feet. At the end of it, Jim called 'Deer on the runway!' and I gave full throttle, carb heat off to allow external air cooling for the engine, and started to climb, gradually releasing the flaps. This is the go-around procedure. I have read where a pilot is not ready to land unless he is prepared to go around. Anything can happen to require a pilot to abort the landing and go around for another try. It could be that the approach is too high, too fast, someone or something is on the runway, gusty winds or anything else that might make the pilot uncomfortable about the landing.

Jim demonstrated a power-off stall, which was not exactly the way I thought it would feel. I thought, as many people do, that the engine quits in a stall. Actually, a stall occurs when the air stops flowing smoothly over the wing surfaces regardless of speed. Jim made the recovery look so easy that I was confident I could do it.

We headed back to the airport and Jim talked me through the traffic pattern. We entered at a 45 degree angle and intercepted the downwind for runway 19. Once abeam the numbers on the runway, I cut power back to 1700 rpm, put carb heat on, added 10 degrees of flaps, turned base, descended and turned final. I was too high and descending too fast, so Jim took over until we were safely on the ground. I think I could do that with some practice.

It was a great day to fly, very smooth and clear. I'm much more comfortable with the controls and I'm getting the feel of the airplane. Can't wait to get back up!

Monday, October 6, 1997 Total Hours: 3.4

I'm not sure why I was concerned, but I was somewhat apprehensive of the required medical exam. My eyesight isn't what it used to be and

I wear reading glasses at times. Maybe that was it, or the fact that I'm over 40 and anything could turn up. I previously got a doctor's name from the Internet (AVWeb) and made an appointment. The doctor has to be an Aviation Medical Examiner (AME) authorized by the FAA. I filled out the forms for new patients and the Application for Student Pilot Certificate and waited.

The exam consisted of a urine test and a routine physical examination including eyesight (which was marginal but OK), blood pressure, respiration, hearing, poking, prodding, tapping, a look in the ears, throat and a hernia check. The only uncomfortable part was getting undressed and wearing that silly robe. Once done, the doctor completed my certificate and gave me further instructions.

The certificate is both a class III medical certificate on one side and the student pilot certificate on the other. There are three classes of medical certificates and all pilots must have one. The class I is the most comprehensive and is required for airline pilots. The class II certificate is required for non-airline, commercial pilots. A private pilot is required to have at least a class III. Because I'm over the age of 40, my medical certificate must be renewed every two years.

The doctor explained, "The student pilot certificate is required for student solo flight, once an instructor endorses it. Later on, when you get the private pilot certificate, the student pilot portion will have no meaning. You cannot carry passengers until you get the private license."

He said "Have fun, be safe and that'll be $50!" One more hurdle overcome.

Thursday, October 9, 1997 Total Hours: 3.4

I performed the preflight ritual as usual and taxied out to the runup area. During the runup, the pilot holds the brakes and increases the throttle to a specified rpm and checks the magnetos. Most good lawn mowers have magnetos to provide a spark to ignite the fuel in the cylinders. That's what makes the engine run. An airplane has two magnetos (a right one and a left one) per cylinder for performance and to provide a backup in case one fails. They are quite important and must be checked before takeoff.

The right magneto checked out but the left one dropped about 300 rpm and made the engine run rough. Jim tried to lean the mixture and burn out any deposits that might be on the spark plugs and tried it again, but did not have any success. I was really disappointed as we taxied over to the mechanic area and parked it. Rats!

There is a hidden lesson in this that is probably more valuable than flying today. The lesson is not to allow your desire to fly, for whatever reason, to cloud your good judgment. My inexperience, coupled with my intense desire to fly, might have caused me to overlook this minor magneto malfunction. The result could have been an unexpectedly short flight ending in a neighborhood near the airport.

Saturday, October 11, 1997 Total Hours: 4.5

Today, during the runup, the magnetos performed magnificently. I executed most of the takeoff but didn't pull up fast enough. I was doing about 80 mph when Jim finally pulled us off the ground. Jim suggested I put slight back pressure on the yoke to pull the nose wheel off the ground at about 50 mph then a little more back pressure at around 60 mph. Once off the ground, nose the plane down slightly to pick up airspeed and climb at about 85 mph. If the pitch attitude is set correctly during the takeoff roll, the airplane will fly so smoothly off the runway that you will hardly discern the difference between the awkward ground beast and the graceful flying machine.

We did a climb, a descent (I remembered carb heat), and rectangular flight around some roads near the Ravenna Arsenal (the practice area). This was a new maneuver for me and one that is on the practical test.

Rectangular course flying simulates the landing pattern at a safe altitude. You pick a field and fly a rectangle around it keeping an equal distance from each side of the field. This can be tricky when the wind is blowing. If it's windy, you have to adjust to compensate. The idea is to turn the airplane toward the wind just enough so that your ground track is a straight line. It's like crossing a river in a boat. If the current is flowing left to right, you have to compensate to the left to maintain a straight line to the other side of the river.

We also performed S-turns, another practical test maneuver. To fly an S-turn, pick a long straight road or railroad and fly an "S" pattern across it, a half circle to the left and then a half circle to the right. Each half should be the same radius and again, compensate for any wind. It's not as easy as it sounds. In addition, you have to maintain the same altitude within plus or minus a hundred feet.

Next, we cruised back to the airport for two landings and one takeoff. I followed directions on the approach and Jim took it at the end. I think it will take some experience to know too high from too low. We focused on the football field at the high school as a reference when flying parallel to the runway. Not every airport has a football field conveniently located on the downwind, so any target landmark will do. I need to remember to trim after each flap setting change during the approach.

It was a good day and I felt like we were making progress. I scheduled flights for the remainder of October and first couple of weeks in November.

Thursday, October 16, 1997 Total Hours: 5.5

I wasn't sure I'd be able to fly today because it got very cloudy, but the clouds were overcast at 4500 feet with a few at 3500. Even though it had been less than a week, it seemed like it had been a long time since I had flown. Jim sent me to the hangar to preflight while he finished with another student.

We taxied out (he said that I go too fast and use too much brake) to runway 01. I got a better feel for the takeoff and climb out. We went east over I-76 to the practice area and did a 360 degree clearing turn. Clearing turns are used to scan the area for other traffic, obstacles and potential emergency landing sites. Next we did some Dutch roll turns to get used to the rudder.

Dutch rolls are strange. The yoke is applied as if to turn and then rudder is applied in the opposite direction to prevent the turn. The result is that you fly a straight path but with the airplane tilted to one side. This simulates what is required for a crosswind landing and it is best practiced at altitude.

We practiced slow flight and a simulated engine out. This is when the instructor pulls the power to idle when you least expect it. Amazingly the airplane still flies, or glides. The purpose is to practice gliding toward a suitable landing area, like a field or an airport, and set up for an emergency landing as if the engine had really failed. In the meantime, don't panic. Follow the procedures to see if you can get the engine started again. There are several things to check that must be committed to memory.

I must study what to do in various emergencies. With power out, we talked about things to try and picked out a field to land on. We descended to about 1000 feet and then did a go-around. It still isn't natural to descend and I seem to fight it.

We did a power-off stall and then headed back. On the way, Jim explained what to do during an electrical failure. I handled more of the radio this time. We descended to 2000 feet and entered the pattern on the crosswind leg. This was just a little north of the airport. Jim let me choose when to turn downwind and I radioed our action.

At a non-towered airport, it isn't required to communicate using the radio, but it is a great safety precaution. You don't know if anyone is listening to what you say, but you say it anyway. If anyone is in the area, they'll know where to look for you. An example of a radio call is "Kent State traffic, Cessna 2497Y is turning final for runway 19, Kent State."

During the landing, I felt much more in control during the descent and turn to base and even during the turn to final. I should have used trim after each flap setting change because the airspeed was erratic. We lined up, cut power and floated down. It didn't feel exactly right when we landed and we were off to one side. I was in control until just before the threshold and then was overwhelmed with all the things to do.

Each time I fly I get a better feel for the airplane and am anxious to fly more often. The process seems to be going slower than I would like, but I guess I need to be patient and it will come.

Saturday, October 18, 1997 Total Hours: 6.6

A good day for flying. I did the takeoff, remembering to lift the nosewheel during the takeoff roll. It was a little off center but not bad. We did a rectangular course, S-turns and a new maneuver, turns around a point.

They are fun. A point on the ground is chosen, like a tree, an intersection or a prominent structure, and the object is to fly a continuous circle around it, maintaining the same distance and altitude. I really messed up the turns around a water tower because I was too close and made too tight a turn.

S-turns were very erratic too, but they got a little better. We did a power-off landing at Portage County runway 09. I controlled most of the landing but didn't level off and pull the yoke back far enough and Jim took over so we wouldn't crunch the nose wheel. He was very particular about this.

We also practiced slips by holding left aileron and hard right rudder. This produced a fast descent with little airspeed change by presenting the side of the airplane to the relative wind. The plane actually went sideways through the air. Weird feeling!

We entered the Kent State pattern on the crosswind leg, and Jim let me pick the distance from the runway. This is a judgment call that is learned only by experience. You don't want to be too close requiring a steep, diving turn to the runway and yet you don't want to be so far away that you couldn't make the runway if the engine quit. I read somewhere to visualize the correct distance by lining up the runway to be about halfway up the strut when you are level at pattern altitude. That seems to work well.

I set up for the approach with kind of a sloppy base turn and was a little slow adding the flaps. Once I was lined up with the runway on final and feeling good about my position, Jim yelled "Deer on the runway!" Time to go-around. I applied full power, carb heat off, increased pitch and let up the flaps slowly. I was pleased that I reacted the way I was taught.

We entered the pattern again for runway 01, and I did everything better this time. I trimmed and maintained the proper airspeed, cut the throttle, leveled off but still didn't pull back hard enough. The stall warning horn came on, as it should, just before we touched down, but, the landing was a little flat.

I told Jim I thought I was over-controlling, especially in the S-turns and turns around a point and that it seemed like I was working hard. He said that is normal and that it really is work to do those maneuvers. Overall, he said I was doing fine. Jim didn't know it but that little bit of encouragement went a long way with me.

After we put the airplane in the hangar, I went over to the classroom area and got familiar with the private pilot test software. This particular software is published by Jeppesen. It does a good job simulating the actual written test. You can drill on required topic areas or take a sample test which selects questions from different areas at random. After some study, I took a sample test and scored 85%. Not bad! I guess my studying is paying off, at least for the test.

The questions that will appear on the written test are not secret, although there has been recent discussion about not making them generally available. I had previously downloaded all the written test questions from the FAA Internet site into my computer. I'm kind of a techno-weenie and built a little data base so that I could practice the test. There are several hundred questions in total, but only 60 will be used on the actual written test. Of course, you don't know which 60 you'll get so you have to be prepared for all of them.

You must to get 70% correct to pass but my goal is 100%. We'll see. Another goal is to get the test over with early. The results are good for two years and I certainly plan to have my license before two years are up.

Once the world realizes that you are a student pilot, you'll receive lots of mail promising to help you pass the written exam. There are videos, books, test booklets, software programs and crash courses available for a price. Whatever you do, make sure the material is current. The questions are changed periodically to reflect changes in regulations and other areas of aviation.

It doesn't do any good to memorize that answer A is the correct answer to a particular question. The answers are scrambled on the real test. The best thing to do is learn the material and the test will seem easy. Don't try to beat the system. Most of the questions are pertinent to your flying. It isn't wise to pass the test and then forget all the information. First, you'll need the knowledge in order to pass the oral exam and second, you need the knowledge to fly safely and within the regulations.

Thursday, October 23, 1997 Total Hours: 7.7

A good day to fly! Jim and I worked on climbing and descending at a fixed speed, steep turns, emergency landings and climbing turns and descents. For the first time we worked with the map and picked landmarks. Up to this time, I always assumed that Jim knew where we were and how to get back to the airport. It dawned on me that I was so busy flying the airplane that I had no clue as to where we were. Comparing the map to what I saw out the window was an education. I learned that some things make great landmarks and others do not. Lake Erie is a good landmark. It's hard to miss. On the other hand, a power line that is so clearly depicted on the map is very difficult to see from the air.

I did three takeoffs and landings all with help from Jim, but I'm starting to get the feel of the pattern, descending and touchdown. Jim said, for this airplane, to fly 90 mph on downwind descent, 80 on base and 70-75 on final. Jim also wants me to be able to convert miles per hour to knots per hour since most newer airplanes use knots per hour on the airspeed indicator.

I still don't quite have the touch for the flare and touchdown, but I'm getting closer. This evenings' takeoffs were to the south. A few miles away I could see the Goodyear Blimp floating peacefully across the sky on its way to the World Series game in Cleveland.

Saturday, October 25, 1997 Total Hours: 8.9

Whew! I'm tired. Today we did nothing but pattern work. Ten take-offs and landings. I was not consistent on the takeoffs due to poor rudder control but they weren't too bad. I'm letting too much speed build up before I pull up. Landings were quite erratic. I can handle the pattern, in fact, Jim said I did excellent pattern work with carb heat, throttle control, flaps, speed control and turns.

My problem starts at about twenty feet from the ground. I have a tendency to over-steer with the ailerons and under-steer with the rudder. I need to line up sooner on the runway during final, stabilize and probably use a little trim. Gentle rudder adjustments are what is needed and pull straight back on the controls without adding any bank. It was grueling, more mentally than physically, and will take some additional practice. It was still very enjoyable and I'm ready to go again. This lesson was 1.2 hours, the longest yet!

Sunday, October 26, 1997 Total Hours: 8.9

I was scheduled for 2:00 P.M. but the weather was bad. I picked up a few video tapes and went home. Maybe tomorrow.

Monday, October 27, 1997 Total Hours: 8.9

Jim called at 7:00 A.M. and we canceled the morning lesson because of weather. He called me later to see if I was interested in some ground lessons. I went to the airport and we talked for a half hour and I took another practice test. I scored 95%. Jim said he'd sign off for me to take the test whenever I think I'm ready. I think I'll do it soon and get it out of the way. I have heard that, if you do well on the written test, the oral exam goes easier.

Now I feel like I'm making progress. I've learned basic maneuvers, passed the medical and accelerated my studies. I've learned a lot about the basics of handling the airplane. I've grown to trust Jim and that is extremely important to me. He is an excellent pilot. Jim said he thought I would get my license at 50-60 hours and that I am doing well. It's become clear that I'll have to really invest a significant amount of time for book work because I won't learn it all in the airplane.

I'm still a rookie but I've noticed that my nervousness is changing to excitement. I'm still a little apprehensive about descending though. I tend to resist pushing the nose over and purposefully flying toward the ground. My control of the airplane is very mechanical with no finesse, too. I expect conditions to be the same each time but I'm learning that conditions are almost never the same. The wind, clouds, temperature and humidity make every flight different. Flying is about adapting to constantly changing conditions and I haven't yet figured out what is really important to pay attention to and what isn't. I tend to 'over-think' each task. It seems that there is so much to think about and I am over-whelmed and consequently forget something important.

I've begun to explore a vast array of aviation resources like DUATS (for weather information), the FAA web site for knowledge test questions and advisory circulars, Internet newsgroups like rec.aviation.student, AVWEB.com, flight simulators and a local phone number for a quick weather briefing. I've also become a big fan of the Weather Channel on TV. The amount of free information available is incredible.

I bought two excellent books to supplement my Jeppesen training materials. The first is *The Student Pilot's Flight Handbook* by William Kershner. Mr. Kershner has a way of explaining things in a simple, efficient and readable manner. The second book has been around since 1944. It's called *Stick and Rudder* by Wolfgang Langewiesche. In order to really understand how an airplane flies, this book explains the concepts of flight in terms that you can relate to.

SOLO!

I remember that first time Dad gave me the car keys and allowed me to take the family car by myself. I recall feeling so proud and independent as I pulled away in that 1964 Ford Fairlane. I just knew that I was the best driver on the road. I had been looking forward to that day and played it over and over in my mind. I was inwardly scared, but I couldn't let it show.

Flying an airplane solo is a major milestone in the learning process and it generates the same feelings of fear and excitement as that first solo drive. At 16 years of age I feared little. At 42, I fear nearly everything. I know too much about responsibility and the consequences of what could happen. I know I'll have to overcome this if I'm going to get past this hurdle. I also know that, at my level of experience, I'm not nearly ready to solo.

I get chills thinking about watching my daughter drive off for the first time. Now I know how Dad felt. Proud and scared. I imagine that's how a flight instructor must feel when he endorses a student pilot for solo flight. Lives are at stake!

Thursday, October 30, 1997 Total Hours: 9.9

It was a great day to fly. We did a review of the maneuvers, like turns around a point, S-turns, steep turns (45 degree bank) left and right and a go-around. I did OK on the turns but had trouble maintaining altitude and I have a tendency to turn too sharp. Steep turns make you feel like you are going to slide out the door of the airplane.

We did two takeoffs and landings and the second landing was much better. It's coming slowly but a little frustrating because it isn't more automatic. I still seem to work too hard at it. I worked on lining up with the center line on approach and my second takeoff was really good. I need to put the nose down a little sooner after takeoff to pick up speed, but still the takeoffs were good. We reviewed some emergency procedures and Jim said I did very well.

He's going to reduce the amount of coaching that he does to set up a maneuver and have me do more of it. Jim says we'll do a few more lessons like this and then I'll take the pre-solo written test. Then I can solo.

Soloing is a scary thought at this point. Some super-humans do it with only 10 hours of experience. I don't feel nearly ready to even think about it. Jim told me earlier that when a student can do three good landings in a row, he's ready to solo. He said a student can luck out once or twice, but not three times in a row.

Friday, October 31, 1997 Total Hours: 10.9

Another good day to fly. We had good wind from the west. We did slow flight, which is coming easier now, and stalls. I set up a full power-off stall and recovered but did a little bit too much release and pulled back too soon. It was much better than the last one I tried. Jim demonstrated a power-on stall and then I did one and recovered very well. It's an odd feeling to be going full throttle at a steep climb angle. It can pin you to the back of your seat. It seems funny to think that a little single engine Cessna can do that. It gets very quiet and then the full stall causes the nose to drop. It was actually fun!

We played a little bit with the VOR indicator (a navigation radio) to see how it works and then returned for landing. After a cruising descent to the pattern altitude we headed in on the 45 degree entry to runway 19. For the first time that I'm aware of, we crabbed into the wind (flying slightly cockeyed) toward the airport then turned downwind. I was a little slow in setting up the first approach and my airspeed got low. It was an OK landing but the second one was much better. After a smooth takeoff, we stayed in the pattern and returned to land. I did all the radio calls, descended smoothly and touched down softly a little right of center line. It was the best landing I've done yet and I don't think I had much help from Jim.

I must remember to steer with the rudders, not ailerons when we're in the flare and line up on center line by looking farther down the runway during the final approach. I was pleased with today's flight. I noticed that taxiing is becoming more automatic and preflight, runup and takeoff are becoming much more natural. Jim said I should review for the pre-solo written test and, if we can't fly tomorrow, I can take the test.

Saturday, November 1, 1997 Total Hours: 10.9

Darn! The weather was marginal. After checking the weather, we decided not to fly due to clouds at 800 feet above the ground in the area. I took the pre-solo written test and did very well. I didn't use any books and only answered a couple of questions incompletely. Jim signed it off and put a little smiley-face on my paper. He told me that on November 15, he won't be available and that I will either fly with Dave, another instructor, or fly solo. He said I'll be ready by then. I hope he knows what he's talking about.

Sunday, November 2, 1997 Total Hours: 10.9

It seems that whenever I schedule several flights in a row, they never work out. Today the weather was marginal with low clouds and gusting winds. We decided that we'd try it in the pattern. I went out and opened the hangar while Jim checked the winds at the airport office. The Hobbs was off by about 9 hours and when I started the preflight, I discovered that the master switch had been left on and the battery was dead. That was the deciding factor. Oh well, maybe next time. Very disappointing. I went back to the office and took another practice test and scored 93.

I'm scheduled for Wednesday at 4:00 P.M. but I'm not sure that I can get away from work. We'll see.

Wednesday, November 5, 1997 Total Hours: 12.2

Luckily, I did get away from work. I called the airport and canceled around 10:00 A.M. A few minutes later I talked to my boss and then called to un-cancel.

The lesson was great! I am much more comfortable in the airplane. I can taxi and talk and listen at the same time! We departed runway 01 with little or no wind. My first takeoff was too abrupt and not enough right rudder. I should have been on the center line and didn't use enough rudder to stay centered, then I pulled back too hard and scared Jim. The other takeoffs were fine. We did slow flight, power-off stalls, steep turns to the right (excellent) and left (lost about 300 feet, not so good). As we navigated back to the airport, we worked on engine emergencies. I think I've got it: carb heat on, mixture rich, fuel on both tanks, magnetos on both, primer in and locked. I thought it was interesting that the pilot should pop the doors open just before an emergency landing. That's so that if the frame gets bent you can still get out.

Next we did three patterns. The first landing was not great. I veered off to the right and landed crooked, not enough rudder and I flared too high. The next approach was good but there was an airplane still on the runway (not a problem) and I should have anticipated that Jim would call 'go-around'. OK, I need to get the flaps out sooner. The next landing was better but I quit too soon. After the wheels touch down, you still have to maintain back pressure on the yoke to reduce speed and slowly release back pressure to ease the nose wheel down. The last one was near perfect. I successfully used rudder to steer and the approach and touchdown were pretty good.

I told Jim that I really enjoy this. It's not the physical flying but the skill building and challenge that are really enjoyable. It was a great evening to fly, too. The last landing was done with the lights and it was getting dark. I could log 1.3 more hours in the book.

I called a Sylvan Learning Center to schedule the written test and Jim said he'd endorse me. It's scheduled for November 20 at 6:00 P.M. in Akron. My next flight is scheduled for Saturday at noon. I hope work doesn't get in the way.

Saturday, November 8, 1997 Total Hours: 12.2

Today's weather was rainy and windy with low clouds. Jim wrote my signoff to take the written exam and I went to work. Maybe tomorrow.

I bought a scanner at Radio Shack to listen to Air Traffic Control (ATC). This proved to be very helpful in learning the phraseology that pilots and controllers use and I'd recommend this as a learning device. I even made my own UHF antenna out of coat hangers and hung it in the attic for better reception. I'm close enough to hear the approach controllers at Akron-Canton Regional Airport, about 15 miles south of Akron, and sometimes I can hear the tower. I can almost always pick up the transmissions from the airplanes.

Sunday, November 9, 1997 Total Hours: 13.2

Clouds today were at 1700 feet with a wind of about 10 knots gusting to 15 knots out of the northwest. It was quite an experience. On runup the left magneto was running rough. Jim ran the rpm up and leaned it a little and it was fine. We stayed in the pattern and did 6 takeoffs and landings. Each one was markedly different as the wind changed. It pushed us around and up and down. I guess these could be exciting with a little more practice. As soon as we climbed above the tree line to the west of the runway, we were blown sideways. According to Jim, holding the aileron into the wind and landing on the windward wheel first is a good way to handle crosswind landings. We approached at faster than normal speeds and used only 20 degrees of flaps. Jim grabbed the controls on a couple of landings and they were interesting to say the least. On one landing it was full right rudder to get lined up.

I think practicing this type landing will make normal landings a little easier. I felt much more comfortable in the pattern today, watching for traffic, using the radio, carb heat, power back, flaps and turns. I even lined up with the runway on final. Then, the wind really came into play. Quick drops, pushes to the side, and sometimes the wind kept us from descending.

I bought a copy of the FAR/AIM for 1998. This publication has the pertinent regulations and Aeronautical Information for pilots. It's very useful to have.

Wednesday, November 12, 1997 Total Hours: 14.3

I wasn't sure I could get away from work today, but it worked out. The sky was clear but it was windy. When I got to the airport I checked the weather and found winds from 280 degrees at 11 knots. Jim said it would be a good day for crosswind takeoffs and landings. We did the pattern about 8 times and, overall, I thought they were good. I need to take out the ailerons a little more as speed builds up to avoid turning right after takeoff. On a couple of takeoffs, the airspeed indicator didn't work until we were off the ground. It probably had a drop of water in it. This confused me the first time. I didn't realize how much I depended on that instrument during takeoff. I knew I was fast and should have pulled up when it felt right instead of relying on the instrument. The second takeoff was better. The landings were fair considering there was a crosswind. On one round, Jim pulled the power and we did a simulated engine out. It was really uneventful.

After the lesson I told Jim that I knew how much I was doing, but I didn't have a good feel for how much he was helping me. He said he did very little, which boosted my confidence a bit. Hopefully, I can solo soon. I'm getting anxious! Next Saturday I will fly with Dave because Jim will be away.

Saturday, November 15, 1997 Total Hours: 14.3

I was supposed to fly with Dave, but the weather didn't cooperate. Snow, low clouds and wind prevented us from flying. Maybe tomorrow will be better.

Sunday, November 16, 1997 Total Hours: 14.3

The weather had improved a little but not enough to fly.

Thursday, November 20, 1997 Total Hours: 14.3

I took the written exam at the Sylvan Learning Center in Akron. My palms were sweaty as I contemplated pressing the 'enter' key to get instant results of my test. I thought about it for a couple of minutes and finally mustered up the courage to do it. I scored 97%! Now that's a load off my mind! I had been working day and night on a project at work and had virtually no study time for the last two weeks. Fortunately I was able to study last night. My practice test average was 95% so I felt ready. I really wanted 100%, but I guess 97% isn't too bad. I missed a question about HIWAS (Hazardous Inflight Weather Advisory Service) frequency. To me none of the answers were right. Maybe Jim can explain it. Now I can quit worrying about studying for the test and concentrate on flying. If I can get in the air, that is.

Sunday, November 23, 1997 Total Hours: 15.0

The wind was blowing from the west at 10 knots. Jim and I went anyway, since I hadn't been in the airplane for more than a week. We did the pattern five times and I think Jim did a lot of the work at touchdown. It's coming a little easier now and certainly seems to be happening more slowly than the first few landings seemed. We talked about how I've reached a plateau and need to move on to the next phase. I'm ready to solo and can't wait to get over that hurdle. I signed up for several more times in December, knowing that I'll probably only get to fly about a third of them due to bad weather.

Saturday, November 29, 1997 Total Hours: 15.0

Canceled due to weather.

Sunday, November 30, 1997 Total Hours: 15.0

Canceled due to weather.

Thursday, December 4, 1997 Total Hours: 15.2

My lesson for today was scheduled for 8:00 A.M. The weather was marginal. There was a low ceiling with a few clouds at 1300 feet. The sky cover was broken at 1900 feet. Jim wasn't there at 8:05 A.M. and because I thought it was doubtful that I could fly, I decided to leave for work. As I was leaving, Jim pulled in and said it looked good enough for pattern work. We checked the weather again and it indicated that it was good enough.

We went out to the hangar and the airplane was not there! It was in for maintenance. Jim said if it was all together, we'd take it out of the maintenance shop. It was fine so I preflighted inside the heated maintenance area which was nice. I taxied out to the runup area and every thing checked out fine. With a slight crosswind from the west, I did a reasonable takeoff. At about 400 feet above the ground Jim took over the controls because the ceiling was actually lower than reported. He landed it and I taxied back to the hangar. Total flight time about 5 minutes. Oh well, maybe Saturday.

Saturday, December 6, 1997 Total Hours: 15.2

Canceled due to weather. Snow with a low ceiling.

Sunday, December 7, 1997 Total Hours: 15.2

Canceled due to low ceiling and poor visibility.

Tuesday, December 9, 1997 Total Hours: 16.3

Finally, I'm back in the air. I did pattern work. Seven times around with one go-around. One was a simulated engine out, which I handled with no problem. There was a slight crosswind from the east and all the landings were fair. I think Jim did very little. I need to focus more on speed control. Takeoffs were very good as the lesson progressed and landings were getting more controlled. I still wanted to jerk the controls around and need to be smoother about all of it. If I could get two more lessons close together, I think I could nail the landings.

All this time off has brought me to the plateau I've heard about. I don't feel like I'm making progress fast enough and it is a little frustrating. Jim is extremely patient with me. I've noticed that we're talking more about the finer points of flying now and I'm not making the big mistakes of the past. I guess I'm getting there. Hopefully, Thursday will be another day like today and then the weekend. The secret for me seems to be flying more often.

Thursday, December 11, 1997 Total Hours: 16.3

The weather was not good. There was a low ceiling, brisk winds and low visibility. Training was canceled.

Saturday, December 13, 1997 Total Hours: 16.3

Jim checked the weather before I got to the airport. It was marginal with a crosswind and low ceiling (2000 feet). He let me decide and I chose not to fly. I've already done two flights with strong crosswinds and it really doesn't let me work on the low wind landings. I think I need to get those down pat before I'm ready to tackle strong winds. Jim agreed and said it was a good decision. Maybe tomorrow will be better.

Sunday, December 14, 1997 Total Hours: 16.3

Canceled again. Low ceiling. This is frustrating.

Tuesday, December 16, 1997 Total Hours: 16.3

At last, a beautiful day for flying! Unfortunately, Jim called last night and told me that he has the flu and can't fly. Canceled again!

Thursday, December 18, 1997 Total Hours: 16.3

Canceled. A clear blue sky but ground fog made visibility less than one mile. For the first time, I considered giving up. How can I expect to make progress if I can't fly. Is Ohio weather always like this? It's frustrating.

Saturday, December 20, 1997 Total Hours: 16.3

Canceled. Another foggy day.

Sunday, December 21, 1997 Total Hours: 17.6

Finally! It's been 11 days and I thought I'd forgotten everything I'd learned. It was a nice day, with winds from the northeast at 9 knots. We went out to the practice area and did clearing turns, turns around a point, Dutch rolls and then pattern work. I still don't quite have the feel of the rudder but its getting better. Landing was really good today and on the first one, I asked Jim if he did anything. He told me he didn't! I did three more after that and they weren't too bad. I have to be getting close to soloing now. This was a fun day!

Monday, December 22, 1997 Total Hours: 17.6

Canceled. Rain and freezing rain. Here we go again.

Tuesday, December 23, 1997 Total Hours: 17.6

Canceled. Low ceiling and light mist with poor visibility.

Tuesday, December 30, 1997 Total Hours: 17.6

Canceled. Snow with low ceiling.

Saturday, January 3, 1998 Total Hours: 18.7

In the air! The wind was about 15 knots from the SSW. We flew seven trips around the traffic pattern. I didn't think it went too bad. Landing and taking off into the headwind was instructive. Flying into a strong headwind makes your ground speed very slow. I realized at this point that it is possible to fly at an indicated air speed of 90 knots and not make any progress in relation to the ground. In fact, it's possible to lose ground! I asked Jim what he would do if he found his ground speed to be extremely low when flying into a strong headwind. He said, "Land."

Tuesday, January 6, 1998 Total Hours: 18.7

Canceled. Low ceiling, broken clouds at 400 feet and 900 feet. Drat!

Thursday, January 8, 1998 Total Hours: 18.7

Canceled. Low ceiling, broken at 300 feet and 800 feet. Drat!

Saturday, January 10, 1998 Total Hours: 18.7

Canceled. Wind 250 degrees 19 knots gusting to 26 knots. Double Drat!

Sunday, January 11, 1998 Total Hours: 19.3

Yes! A relatively calm day and clear. 97Y was not available so I didn't think I'd be able to fly. Jim called just before 3:00 P.M. and said we could get another airplane (N62953) for one hour. We wouldn't have to get it out of the hangar or put it up since it would be out already. It was up to me. I said "Let's go!" We did 3 takeoffs and landings in a light crosswind. I really liked the airplane, too. The gauges were where I could read them and the flaps are electric. It has four cylinders and is much quieter, too. All takeoffs and landings were good despite being unfamiliar with the airplane.

Wednesday, January 14, 1998 Total Hours: 20.8

I SOLOED! What a feeling! The lesson was at 8:00 A.M. on a cloudy but clearing morning. It was crisp with no wind. There were high, bright, puffy, white clouds against a backdrop of crystal clear blue sky. Every time I see a sky like that, I smile to myself and remember this day. I preflighted as normal and taxied out to runway 01. After the runup, Jim and I did six takeoffs and landings with one go-around. On about the fifth time around, Jim told me that I need to solo soon and if I didn't have to go to work, this would be a good day to do it. If I didn't do it today, the next time out we would go up in the pattern a few times, stop and he would sign me off and I'd solo then. I said "To heck with work, let's do it!" And we did. All the previous landings were pretty good. Jim quizzed me on my position, high or low, left or right, fast or slow. I've really acquired a feel for my position.

After we landed for the sixth time, we parked by the FBO (Fixed Base Operation, the airport office) and went inside. Jim signed off my log book and student pilot certificate. He sent me out to do an abbreviated preflight then joined me in a few minutes. We started up and headed to runway 01. As we were taxiing, another airplane was back-taxiing toward us. I had the right of way but turned around anyway and we did the runup on the 19 end of the runway. Everything checked out and I taxied down to the end of runway 01 and stopped. There was an airplane in the pattern and one behind me doing his runup.

Jim got out in the 17 degree weather and I was on my own! I waited for the arriving airplane to land (touch and go) and announced my departure, taxied out and I was off! Full power is much faster without Jim and I was in the air in no time. I climbed out with my heart pounding and a million thoughts running through my head. My main thought was that I was off the ground and *only I* could safely land the airplane again. I also thought about how big the airplane seemed without someone sitting next to me. About 500 feet off the ground I let out a war-whoop at the top of my lungs! I wondered if anyone heard me. I had to keep telling myself to relax and fly the airplane. I steepened the climb, watched for other traffic and radioed my turn to crosswind. I was too fast and high so I made the necessary adjustments. I remember thinking, "I really do know enough to do this!" I had to extend my downwind leg until the other airplane in the pattern passed by on it's final. I turned to base and final a little high and fast but the approach was OK. I flared and reduced throttle but brought the nose up too fast and ballooned. Ballooning happens when you pull back on the yoke too much or too fast and the airplane starts to climb again. I caught it and landed a little long but safely down the middle. WHEW! One down, two to go.

The second was better than the first because I maintained speed better. The third was, in my opinion, excellent! I even made the first exit off the runway. Fantastic! I told Jim on the way back in that I was confident and was never in doubt about anything. He was so frozen from the cold that he probably didn't comprehend my babbling. For the next few days, I couldn't stop grinning from ear to ear everytime I thought about what I had done. I am so proud of my accomplishment. I told everyone who I thought might be remotely interested! Wow!

At this stage, the feeling of accomplishment is indescribable. I've come a long way. I've learned to taxi, passed the written exam, and got much better at landing. I seriously considered giving up because I was frustrated with all the bad weather and felt I had reached a point where I was making little or no progress. I'm very glad I didn't!

Jim was extremely patient and seemed to understand exactly how I felt. He did a great job building my confidence and preparing me to fly solo. He seemed to know when I was ready. I was no longer a pre-solo rookie. I was on my way to being a real pilot!

Late in his life, Dad would tell a story to his friends and family about something one of his sons had accomplished. His voice would crack a little and his lips would quiver and you could see his pride pour out of his tear blurred eyes. I still get a lump in my throat just thinking about how pleased he would have been to share this moment with me.

I know he was with me.

Building Flying Skills

Now that I think about it, those solo trips around the traffic pattern were like driving a car around the block for the first time. Significant, but such a small part of the overall picture. The next series of lessons presented a number of new experiences and the opportunity to build consistency with the basic skills.

I have much better control of the airplane and it is becoming more automatic. The ability to control an airplane must become automatic in order to be able to function in the flight environment.

Monday, January 19, 1998 Total Hours: 20.8

Canceled. The weather was good but we had a little snow the day before. The runway was being plowed when I got to the airport and we decided that it would be too icy for safe flight.

Thursday, January 22, 1998 Total Hours: 21.7

Very interesting! When I got to the airport around 4:00 P.M., Jim said the airplane we scheduled to fly had some problems that were being fixed. We would take the next best airplane at the same cost. He gave me choices today. We could either fly to Akron-Canton Regional a towered, Class C airport, work on special takeoffs and landings or something else I wanted to work on. Since it was a different airplane (N54064), I thought I'd get the most out of visiting a class C airport. What a trip! We listened to ATIS (Automatic Terminal Information Service) while on the ground at Kent (they give each update a letter identifier, this one was information "Papa").

I then took off from runway 19 and headed south. A couple of miles away from Kent we called Akron Approach on the radio. They acknowledged us and said they had us on radar. We would be landing on runway 01 with a right hand pattern. The controller advised us of traffic to our 11 o'clock position. It was the Goodyear blimp going in for a landing at the blimp hangar near the airport. It was quite a sight seeing the blimp from the top as we flew over it. When we were down-wind of runway 01, there was some confusion and the controller told us to turn left away from the runway. It looked to the controller like we were setting up to land on runway 32, which was closed. Once this was cleared up, we were cleared to land on runway 01, which we did. Wide runways! It was great seeing the big jets parked at the terminal, small jets taxiing around and me in my Cessna putt-putt-ing down the runway!

We taxied off the runway under instructions from the controller, held short at runway 05, then, when cleared to cross, we did. We told the controller what we wanted to do next and received instructions to follow the Lear jet to runway 01. After the jet took off, so did we. We followed heading 050 away from the airport and then turned North. When we could see the runway at Kent State, we informed departure control and they terminated radar service. Next we called up Kent and got the airport advisory and landed normally.

There was a lot of communication going on up there and I'm sure that this was not a busy time for the airport. I have a lot to learn about anticipating what the controller will say next and listening to the instructions. I'm sure glad Jim was there!

Saturday, January 24, 1998 Total Hours: 21.7

We canceled flying due to low ceiling and icing conditions. We got in 1.5 hours of ground lessons including weight and balance calculations plus cross country planning. Jim also answered my questions about crosswind landings (use of rudder) and speed control on approach. He said we'll work next on short field and soft field takeoffs and landings, cross country, maneuvers and solo work. I picked up a current Detroit sectional (map) and a Cleveland terminal chart.

Sunday, January 25, 1998 Total Hours: 22.6

Jim said we would work on specialty takeoffs and landings but since there was a crosswind at Kent State we would go to Akron-Fulton airport, about 10 miles south, to practice. We took off runway 01 and circled around. The ceiling got lower as we went south. We landed on runway 25 at Akron-Fulton and then taxied back to the start of runway 25.

We did a short field takeoff with 10 degrees flaps. Full power is applied while holding the brakes on and then you let go. You pick up speed quickly and after takeoff you climb steeply. Once you've cleared the FAA standard 50 foot imaginary tree you lower the nose and pick up speed and climb out normally. We circled around and the ceiling was getting much lower with light snow. We navigated back to Kent and landed on runway 01. We finished with one more takeoff and landing.

All my landings were not very good. I was trying to think about left aileron and right rudder at the expense of staying down the runway centerline. I need to practice this now that I have the general idea of how it's done.

Tuesday, January 27, 1998 Total Hours: 23.8

Good news and bad news. The ceiling today was about 3500 feet with a little wind from the east. Jim said we would fly to the practice area and do a phase check. We took off using the short field takeoff and then headed out. We did clearing turns followed by steep turns at 3000 feet. Next we did power-off stalls and power-on stalls. I couldn't get the airplane to fully stall with power on and neither could Jim. We reviewed emergency electrical procedures and a simulated engine failure. I would not have made the field I picked out because I was too high. I have to work on that. We finished with S-turns then headed for home. My S-turns were too steep to start with and that threw me off for the rest of them. I need work there too. Otherwise, every thing was good.

On the way back, Jim turned off the LORAN, a navigation radio, and asked me to find my way home. I followed I-80 until I saw the airport off to the south and headed for it. As we landed, Jim showed me the soft field landing using 1200 rpm all the way to touchdown. I didn't know what to do so I pulled the power out as soon as we touched down. Oops! Jim wasn't pleased that I did that. We took off one more time and did it again. This time I left the power in like I was supposed to!

We taxied back and Jim said I did a really good job today. I walked away with a lot of confidence. Then he hit me with the bad news. He had given his two weeks notice and would be moving on to be a charter pilot in Sandusky, flying to the islands in Lake Erie. I told him I was happy for him and disappointed for me. It sounded like a good opportunity for him and I can't say that I didn't expect this to happen sometime. Jim said we would work on a few more specialty landings and takeoffs and then he would sign me off for solo practice. We had also been planning a dual cross country trip to Franklin, Pennsylvania. We really wanted this trip in before he left. If the weather is OK we'll go on Saturday.

Thursday, January 29, 1998 Total Hours: 24.9

Bad weather was predicted but when I got up this morning the ceiling was still high and fairly clear. The prediction was that it would get worse around noon. We worked on soft field takeoffs and landings for about 5 trips around the pattern and then short field takeoffs and landings for 4 trips.

Soft field landings aren't as hard as I imagined they would be. In fact, the landings are softer since power is kept on all the way to the ground. I need more practice but they went fairly well. Jim said I did a good job today and that we'll do the cross country then sign me off for solo practice. I just hope we can do this before he leaves.

Saturday, January 31, 1998 Total Hours: 26.1

Planning a cross country trip involves marking your course on the map, marking checkpoints and calculating wind correction, determining the fuel required and the estimated flight time. The flight plan is filed by calling an 800 number for Flight Services then giving them the details of the plan. You give the airplane tail number, departure time, route, altitude, estimated flight time, fuel on board, name, home base, color of the airplane and number of souls on board. They will start calling for you if you fail to call and close the flight plan after you arrive. If they can't locate you, a Search and Rescue team will be sent out to find the wreckage. I imagine they frown on pilots who forget to close their flight plans.

I had planned and re-planned for the cross country to Franklin and I filed the flight plans about 10:00 A.M. Jim called me just before I left home and asked what the weather was like. The ceilings were 2600 feet at Akron, with the prediction to be 3500 feet later. Franklin ceiling was 1800 feet and there was a report of thin ice on the runway. We chose not to go.

Jim said I could solo or both of us could go in the pattern together for a few landings and then I could solo afterwards. I said I'd like to do a few with him first. We did four and they were OK but not really good.

I dropped him off and soloed for three times around. The first landing was not too bad. I dropped in a little hard but otherwise it was fair. The second one was a little crooked on the runway and I had to straighten out once on the ground. The third one was scary. My approach was fine, but when I got near the ground there was enough crosswind to blow the airplane to the right. I compensated with aileron which cocked me left across the centerline. I didn't get enough right rudder in to straighten out with the centerline and touched down cocked to the left on the right wheel and then on the nosewheel. I thought for a second that I would lose it, but I maintained control and taxied in. I was shaken and my confidence took a severe blow.

Hours later, I still couldn't stop thinking about that landing. Jim said sometimes you just have bad days and that the winds can be tricky on runway 01. Now I question if I'm ready for solo landings. I guess I just have to learn from these occasions and it will help me the next time. I drove home and filled out the papers for aircraft rental insurance ($200.00) and got it ready to mail on Monday. Jim and I are now planning to fly cross country to either Mansfield, OH or Franklin, PA tomorrow.

Sunday, February 1, 1998 Total Hours: 28.2

What a nice day. The sky was clear with a southerly 8 knot wind. I filed my flight plan for Franklin. Jim was flying with another student so I preflighted and got the airplane out of the hangar without him. He came about 12:20 P.M. and we took off. We didn't open the flight plan because Jim said the VOR radio wasn't working. I think he later determined that it wasn't turned on and we could have done it, but by then it was too late.

I found my first checkpoint without any trouble. I found that the winds, and hence my course calculations, were off by about 30 degrees so we made the adjustment and flew on to the rest of the checkpoints.

It's sometimes confusing to try to locate details on the maps. It is a lot easier to see major things such as lakes and interstate highways or airports. I was south of the planned course most of the time but not so far off that I couldn't see the checkpoints and correct my course. We requested VFR flight following in the TRSA (radar service) over Youngstown and flew over the Youngstown airport. There really wasn't as much communication required as I originally thought. The controller told me that Franklin was 9 miles out from my 11:00 o'clock. I saw it and we terminated radar following. I called Franklin and got the active runway, which was 20. I got in the pattern on crosswind and made the landing with Jim's help. I was still a little shaky from yesterday's fiasco.

Although small, Franklin is an excellent airport and facility. We looked around for about ten minutes and then headed back, deciding not to stop in Youngstown on the return flight. I took off on runway 20 and headed west then announced to the Youngstown controller that I was a student pilot. They took it from there. The controller was very helpful. He asked for the type of aircraft and my intentions and let us go on through with no further directions. As we got closer to it, I could easily see the reservoir near Kent and started to pick out familiar landmarks like Portage County airport, the Cuyahoga Falls tower, Akron-Fulton airport, Kent State University and the Ravenna Arsenal.

When we entered the pattern for 19 on a 45 degree angle I got a little flustered. I was initially too low and fast and never really got in the landing groove. I was high on final and decided to go-around. Jim said it was a good decision and so I got set up in the pattern again, the right way, and landed without problem with a slight crosswind from the right. Not a great landing, but certainly better than yesterday. I made it!

Jim said I did a great job handling the navigation and maintaining heading and just did an overall good job. 2.1 hours made this the longest flight yet. After we landed, Jim told me he was going to fly with Fred, another private pilot, to Columbus so he could get more experience at a larger airport and that I could go along if I wanted. I said yes and we cleared it with Fred. We took off and I tracked our course to Columbus and back comparing landmarks to the map. It was such a nice day to fly that even after being in the airplane for two hours on my trip, I really enjoyed flying without the pressure of being the pilot!

I told Jim that my confidence with landings was pretty low after yesterday and he told me that runway 01 is a tough one to solo on. There was a tailwind and a stronger crosswind than when we did the pattern just before my solo. He said we'd work together on landings and that he'd want me to solo after that to build up my confidence. I need that!

Thursday, February 5, 1998 Total Hours: 29.2

Winds were from the north today at 13 knots and were even higher at Portage County. We left Kent and entered a 45 for downwind for runway 27 at Portage County. I crabbed about 30 degrees to stay on the downwind course. Jim told me he would take the first landing to see how strong the wind really was. He really had to fight it so I was glad he did it first. We landed and taxied back. He said 'Now, you do it' and we took off again. With help, I landed and did a better job this time. Jim gave me a choice, do more or go back to Kent and practice into the wind. I chose to go home. We did three more patterns at Kent. None of the landings were great but I learned a little more about rudder control. I'm ready to try it again and am determined to master this phase of the training.

Saturday, February 7, 1998 Total Hours: 30.4

Saturday was a beautiful day, with a 4 knot wind from the north. Jim was out with another student when I arrived so I had the line crew put 97Y on the ramp and did my preflight in the bright sunshine. As I was finishing, Jim came and we prepared to take off. He said we would do a couple of patterns and then I would solo. He wanted me to leave the pattern, do some maneuvers and then return and do practice landings. I haven't been signed off for other airports yet so I couldn't go anywhere else. We did twice around the track, landing on runway 01 (not my favorite). They were beautiful. Smooth touchdown, under control and I made the turnoff on both of them. Jim said the first one was so good, he thought he'd cry!

I taxied back to the runup area on the 19 end and Jim got out. I told him what I was going to do and he said, "Just have the airplane on the ramp at 3:00 P.M." I took off, climbed to 2500 feet and headed east to the practice area. Even though I wasn't landing there, I tuned in the Portage County frequency as I got closer and listened for traffic. I did clearing turns, steep turns and worked on rudder coordination in turns. After a while I headed west toward the Kent State airport. During my maneuvers, an acrobatic airplane passed over in front of me upside down!

I entered the pattern on crosswind after making the approach call and went in for my first landing. Not too bad, but again I got angled off the centerline to the right. Touchdown was good but I was way too close to the side of the runway. The next try was almost exactly the same. Angled to the right, good touchdown, but too far right. I decided to call it quits for today and headed in.

I'm getting my confidence back slowly, but I need more practice! I think I always have to use right rudder and when I need to turn left near the centerline I don't give it enough. I am even more determined!

Sunday, February 8, 1998 Total Hours: 31.3

Another beautiful day, but foggy in the morning. I checked the weather several times and, while the sky was clearing, it wasn't good enough to go anywhere except the pattern. This was fine with me. Jim and I worked on short field and soft field takeoffs and landings and I think it went fairly well. All the landings were smooth and accurate. I don't know what it is about having Jim in the airplane, but it makes things go much better. I guess I'll get used to flying alone eventually.

For a short field takeoff, we lined up at the end of the runway with 10 degrees flaps, locked the brakes and applied full power. That little Cessna sounded pretty mean when it was all wound up and straining to go! I released the brakes and maintained the centerline using rudder control. I also maintained full back pressure until the plane was rolling good then slightly released the back pressure. The airplane virtually took off by itself! I maintained the best angle of climb speed (about 65 mph) until we were clear of the imaginary 50 foot obstacle, then nosed over to pick up speed, established a climb and retracted the flaps.

The object of a soft field takeoff is to takeoff from a muddy or snow-covered runway without getting stuck. To accomplish this, the pilot applies 10 degrees of flaps with full back pressure and rolls out to the runway without stopping. The pilot then applies full power, releases a little back pressure to keep the nose lower, goes to 'flying' speed and then applies back pressure to lift off. He then releases some back pressure to remain relatively low in 'ground effect' until the speed increases to the best climbing speed. Once climbing, the flaps are retracted.

On short field landing, imagine a 50 foot tree near the end of the runway. Approach normally until over the obstruction, apply the remaining 10 degrees of flaps and descend steeper than normal without picking up excessive air speed. Very lightly, touch down with continued back pressure, retract the flaps quickly and apply heavy braking.

For a soft field landing, approach normally, retain 1000-1200 rpm to land very softly and maintain full back pressure until safely off the runway. It's a lot to think about but, with practice, these can be fun!

Monday, February 9, 1998 Total Hours: 32.1

This was a fun day. As we checked the weather, Jim discussed going to the Akron-Canton Regional airport to pick up a couple of radios. So we left Kent State and headed there. I did most of the radio work and actually understood most of the exchanges. We were cleared to land straight in on runway 19 at Akron-Canton. I had never done a straight in approach, but did it just fine. It was a good landing on a very wide runway. We taxied over to Lawrence Aviation and picked up the radios and headed home. Jim coached me through using the radio to get the ATIS, contact ground control and talk to the tower. As we got closer to Kent, radar services were terminated. I called Kent and entered downwind for 19. Jim asked me to do a soft field landing. I didn't do it very well because I was too high and fast on the approach. This seems to be a common problem that I'll have to work on.

Tuesday, February 10, 1998 Total Hours: 32.1

I mailed in the aircraft rental insurance form with a check to the insurance company and it was returned. I was informed they weren't taking these any more. I called Jim and he advised me to become a member of the Aircraft Owners and Pilots Association (AOPA) and get insurance from that organization. As luck would have it, I got a flier from AOPA in the mail the same day. I sent in membership dues of $39 (I got a free hat) and the next day called the insurance part of AOPA. I got the necessary forms and sent in the application with a check for $215. Haven't heard from them yet.

I'm slowly gaining my confidence. It's amazing how quickly I lost confidence and how slowly it comes back. I'm feeling better about being in the air alone but it still produces high anxiety. I tend to get all worked up just thinking about it and then, when I get in the airplane, I settle down and it goes fine.

I'm gaining experience with the cross country trip to Franklin and flying into a tower controlled airport. This is beginning to be more fun than work. My fear and anxiety is turning more to excitement and anticipation.

A New Instructor

The thought of Jim leaving made me a little skeptical of what would happen next in my training. Jim was an excellent pilot and a good instructor and I'd grown to trust his judgment. Now, I'd have to learn to trust someone else. As it turned out, it was probably the best thing for me. I may have grown too comfortable with Jim in the right seat and more dependent on him than necessary. The change happened at a good time in my development.

Saturday, February 14, 1998 Total Hours: 33.1

More short field and soft field takeoffs and landings. I learned how to use trim to control speed on descent and it really helped. None of the landings were real good but they were passable. Jim's last day is tomorrow and it appears that the new guy has a job on the weekends. I don't know what will happen next. I'd signed up for every weekend through March and now it is uncertain if I'll get to fly. Bummer. Jim said we should do a night cross country to Mansfield to get more cross country and night requirements in. We may work on instruments tomorrow. I'm a little depressed about not having an instructor. Jim gave me his new home phone number in Sandusky and told me to call with any flying questions or if I fly into the area, perhaps we could meet for lunch.

Sunday, February 15, 1998 Total Hours: 34.2

Jim's last day. The weather was perfect for pattern work with very light winds from the south. We did soft field and short field takeoffs and landings and then I soloed, doing three trips around the pattern. The first landing was nearly perfect, a real confidence booster! The second was right of the center line but not severely and the third was very good! I needed that and Jim knew it. I paid close attention to my approach speed and angle and it paid off. I used trim to control on downwind, to keep from climbing too much. I also trimmed for speed during descent. I also learned a lesson about right rudder on takeoff. It takes more right rudder just after lift off without Jim in the airplane.

I walked away feeling that I had finally accomplished something. I met Mike, a new instructor, who I am scheduled to fly with tomorrow. It's hard to tell anything about him but he didn't seem, on first impression, to be real confident. I guess that is understandable. He seemed surprised when I told him that I would be in tomorrow at 3:30 P.M.. Another six tenths of an hour of solo for the log book!

Monday, February 16, 1998 Total Hours: 34.2

Canceled due to light rain and a 15 knot crosswind. I called Mike to check if we were flying. I asked him about his availability on the weekends and he said he would try to match my schedule with one of the other instructors. My next flight is scheduled for Saturday. I hope we can work something out.

Saturday, February 21, 1998 Total Hours: 34.2

I met with Bill, my new instructor. Bill will be working Saturday and Sunday with me. Today's flight was canceled due to low ceilings and mist so we did some ground work preparing for a night cross country to Mansfield. Bill suggested that we do some local night flight before we tackle the cross country because I have never flown at night.

We worked out a route following the Akron VOR outbound to the Mansfield VOR inbound and discussed checkpoints and radio use. We also chose to take N54064 instead of 97Y. We covered other points of night flight, weather, lights, navigation and then Bill asked me to plan the flight for the trip. If we can't fly tomorrow, we'll review the flight plan. We walked out to the runway and Bill showed me how to operate the pilot controlled lighting.

When flying at night and need to turn on the runway lights, you tune to the appropriate radio frequency and key the mike 7 times within 5 seconds. Bill had a hand held radio and demonstrated turning the lights on using it. Then we went to the hangar to review the instrument panel. I took the 'Night Flight' video home with me. This should be interesting.

Sunday, February 22, 1998 Total Hours: 35.3

Today's ceiling was at about 3500 feet with a little north wind. This was my first time flying with Bill. Preflight, taxi and runup went fine and I departed runway 01 for the practice area. We did clearing turns and steep turns, slow flight, power-on and power-off stalls and then headed back for three landings and one short field takeoff. The first landing was off to the right, the second was good and the third was off to the left. Bill thinks that I'm coming in too fast, flaring too early and too much. Then I get too slow and the controls don't work as well. So, I should come in a little faster, flare closer to the ground and it should be OK.

Bill is a real stickler for procedure and oral execution of checklists. He says that is what the examiner is going to look for. If you explain what you are doing, the examiner won't ask as many questions.

Bill went to Kent State and learned to fly in 1982. He has a different style than Jim. While Jim was pretty laid back, Bill is quick to criticize and I think this is going to be good for my flying. He demonstrated slow flight during the lesson and later told me that he did this because I didn't use flaps when I did it. I did it because Jim and I practiced this both ways, with and without flaps. Bill explained the reason for slow flight with flaps is to simulate the landing. I understand. Bill demonstrated a power-off stall and we veered off to the left and for a brief second I was worried, but he recovered fine.

Bill isn't as precise about his demonstrations as Jim was but he seems to know what will pass the practical exam and is determined to hold me to the standards required. He asked me to study the checklists and practice saying them. For example, when we start taxiing, he wants me to check the instruments and say, "Airspeed zero, attitude indicator uncaged and erect, altimeter set, VSI at zero, DG indicates a turn, turn coordinator indicates a turn, compass has fluid and indicates a turn. Taxi checklist is complete!" He wants to hear me say what I'm doing at every stage of flying. Its different, more work, not as casual but probably the best thing for me at this time.

Thursday, February 26, 1998 Total Hours: 36.1

Whoa! Yet another humbling experience. Just when you start getting a little comfortable…

Three things were different. First, I flew N54064 which is completely different than good old 97Y. The instruments are in the standard places but 97Y isn't like that. I had a hard time finding anything at a glance. Second, there was a very significant crosswind from the east. I haven't mastered normal landings yet and a stiff crosswind in a strange airplane was tough. Lastly, it was dark!

We did some ground work, discussed the night differences and basically stalled until it was pretty dark outside. I did the preflight with a flashlight. Then we taxied out (I did remember the taxi checklist) and took off with the crosswind. That was ugly.

The first attempt to land ended in a high go-around. I guess that it is normal to avoid going too low when the distance to the ground can't be clearly judged. It takes practice to get used to this. When I turned final on my first attempt I don't think I had descended one foot. I looked down at that tiny sliver of asphalt outlined by red, white and green lights and I knew the only way we could hit the runway would be a nose dive ending in a crash. The go-around option was a wise choice. The next one was high, but I salvaged it. It was not pretty. The last approach was great, but the flare was lousy and the touchdown was hard.

I felt like I had been beaten. Bill gave me a grade for each thing we did during the lesson. He rated me on a scale of 1 to 5 with 1 being excellent and 5 bad. Bill gave me an overall grade of 2 for the day with 3's on the crosswind parts. He was pretty encouraging though. He said I did well under some tough conditions. Whew!

Saturday, February 28, 1998 Total Hours: 36.9

It was overcast and the forecast was for rain, however the ceilings were at 3500 feet and visibility was 3 miles. We decided to go up in the pattern. We practiced short field, soft field, and short-soft field takeoffs and landings and I did well on all of them. There was little wind to deal with and my patterns were all controlled. I remembered to do the checklists during taxi and the pre-landing GUMPS check (*G*as -both tanks on; *U*ndercarriage—wheels down and locked; *M*ixture—rich; *P*ropeller and power set; *S*eat belts on) in the pattern. My speed was well controlled and each landing was precise.

Bill said if the weather was a little better, he'd let me go by myself, but I wasn't able to. Bill gave me a 2 for the day, which is above average. It was fun. We are planning a night flight to Youngstown on Tuesday and will fly tomorrow if the weather permits. Bill says we need a stiff crosswind, but I could do without it.

Sunday, March 1, 1998 Total Hours: 37.6

I soloed! The ceilings weren't high enough to really go anywhere so Bill asked me if I wanted to stay in the pattern. I said OK. He said I could go solo and he'd only help me get the airplane out. OK! We got it out then Bill shut the hangar door and walked back to the office leaving me to do my thing.

I went through the normal routine with the pre-start and verbally went through the taxi checklist. I did the runup and took off on runway 19. There wasn't very much wind for the first landing which was a little rough but acceptable. I taxied back to do it again. The wind picked up a little from the west and got noticeably stronger as I cleared the trees. I got around the pattern in good shape remembering to do the GUMPS check. Carb heat, reduce power, set airspeed and finish the pattern. It was a little rough, but again, acceptable. The next time up I tried a short field takeoff, but forgot the flaps at 10 degrees. I had to stay in ground effect to get enough speed to climb out.

The Goodyear blimp was in front of me about a mile away. I calmly said over the radio, "I have the blimp in sight", and turned crosswind a little earlier than normal to avoid getting too close to it. I set up in the pattern and on final, noticed that I had to crab more into the west wind. I also noticed downdrafts and updrafts on final approach. I approached a little faster than normal and touched down firmly. (Bill told me later that he heard the tires squeal on that one.) OK, one more. I debated whether to go for one more, chose to do it and resolved to make it a good one. The crosswind had picked up. I tried a soft field takeoff with flaps this time, rolling out to the centerline then giving it full power. Just as I took off the stall warning sounded and I lowered the nose to stay in ground effect, picked up speed, climbed and took out the flaps. Not too bad! I climbed to 2000 feet and set up the approach. The plane was in good position on final, crabbing into the wind. I experimented with the left rudder to determine how much to use and found it was a lot. When I did, I drifted a bit to the left and applied right aileron to drift back into the wind. I must have let up on the rudder and drifted back left of centerline. I flared and landed straight, but left of center. Touchdown was soft but the airplane floated a little. I remembered to look farther down the runway and it helped to judge my height from the runway. I need to remember that.

Whew! That was a drain. I taxied back to the fuel pump where Bill met me. The latest Unicom update said an 8 knot crosswind and I had made it! It was mentally and physically draining, but I did it!

After we put the airplane away, Bill and I discussed our Tuesday cross country flight to Youngstown. He said I could possibly fly a solo cross country to Ashtabula next Saturday and to start planning it. A cross country is defined as a flight of at least 50 miles from the point of departure and a landing. I think Ashtabula is 50.1 miles away. I thought it might as well be an Atlantic crossing! Could an airplane really fly that far? Was I ready for this?

Tuesday, March 3, 1998 Total Hours: 37.6

The night flight was canceled due to low ceilings. I called for a weather briefing around noon for a 6:30 P.M. flight to Youngstown and decided that the weather was not good enough. I called the airport and canceled.

Bill's disciplined style has made me a better pilot. I've become much more comfortable with him and feel like I've made progress. I learned not only to trust Bill, but, more importantly, I learned to trust myself.

That first night flight a week ago was one I wouldn't soon forget. I need to work on developing my night flying skills.

CROSS COUNTRY PREPARATION

The second greatest milestone in learning to fly an airplane is to actually fly solo to another airport. A pilot in training is required to accumulate 5 hours of solo cross country time, one of which must be at least 150 miles with three landings. Additional cross country time can be accumulated by flying to another airport at least 50 miles away. Bill and I will take some dual trips before I'm ready to go it alone. I've learned about the flight environment and now must pay closer attention to the weather. Bill's forcing me to make more and more of the decisions and I'm slowly being weened from the reliance I have on an instructor.

Saturday, March 7, 1998 Total Hours: 38.6

What a nice day! It's about 50 degrees with light variable winds. When I got to the airport, Bill asked me if I wanted to fly the cross country to Ashtabula. Nervously, I said yes. He checked the schedule and found out that someone had scheduled the airplane at 2:00 P.M.. He said, "Well, maybe next Saturday."

We flew to the practice area and, at my request, did slips (bank left, hard right rudder, and fly nearly sideways) , rectangular course, turns around a point, S-turns, and an emergency descent then headed back. My landing on runway 01 was not too bad although Bill told me that I ballooned a bit. The stall horn came on but I thought I was about to touchdown and that that was good. Bill said I was still about 3 feet off the ground! Thump.

I quizzed Bill about my progress and how I was doing in relation to the hours that I have accumulated. He said I was doing very well and was right on track with where I should be. He said that flying frequently was the key and I've been able to keep up a good schedule. We looked over my flight plans for Ashtabula and Youngstown. Bill said they looked good. He told me that he was a little nervous on his first cross country and that he got lost. Now I'm even more apprehensive about getting lost and, of course, landing! Other than that, I guess I'm ready. Bill seems to think so too. Maybe next Sunday.

Sunday, March 8, 1998 Total Hours: 38.6

Canceled due to weather.

Tuesday, March 10, 1998 Total Hours: 38.6

Canceled due to weather.

Thursday, March 12, 1998 Total Hours: 38.6

Canceled due to weather.

Saturday, March 14, 1998 Total Hours: 38.6

Canceled due to weather. High winds with low ceilings.

Sunday, March 15, 1998 Total Hours: 38.6

Canceled due to weather. Strange off and on snow showers.

Tuesday, March 17, 1998 Total Hours: 38.6

Canceled due to weather. High winds with low ceilings.

Saturday, March 21, 1998 Total Hours: 38.6

Canceled due to weather. High winds with low ceilings and snow.

Sunday, March 22, 1998 Total Hours: 38.6

Canceled due to low ceilings. Light snow. I did some ground work on flight planning.

Tuesday, March 24, 1998 Total Hours: 40.6

This was a great lesson! Bill and I completed the night cross country to Ashtabula County, Youngstown and back to Kent State. I finished the preflight just as it was getting dark. We departed runway 01 with very little wind. There were no winds aloft forecasted. As we approached I-80, my first checkpoint, I tried to tune in the Chardon VOR for navigation but couldn't pick up the signal. We ended up tuning in the Jefferson VOR and just tracked to it. I couldn't clearly see any of my other checkpoints. With so many lights, everything on the ground looks the same.

As we got close to 7G2 (Ashtabula County airport) I called Unicom and no one answered so we considered the wind and decided to land on runway 26. The landing wasn't too bad as I wasn't nearly as high on the approach as I was during my first night flight. I landed safely, taxied up to the office, turned around and headed back to the runway.

We then took off for Youngstown. Although I could have handled it, Bill did all the radio work around Youngstown. We were vectored around a little and cleared to land on runway 23. Bill told me to turn right and I thought he must have seen the runway. Actually, neither of us had the runway in sight and were too far to the right by the time we saw it. The controller said, "97Y, do you have the runway in sight?" Sheepishly, Bill responded, "No, we missed it." The controller told us to turn left, head away from the airport and follow another plane (a Bonanza) in to runway 32. We saw the other airplane, followed it in and did a stop and go landing. The controller instructed us to spend minimal time on the runway, so we took off again. We lined up on the Akron VOR, but just followed I-80 all the way back. We entered the pattern for runway 01 and landed, not really well, but landed.

It was a very enjoyable two hours. I learned the necessity of knowing where you are and where you are going at night. The sky was crystal clear and yet I had trouble locating and maintaining visual contact with the airports. It all blends together. I thought I would get some real insight into my solo cross country to Ashtabula, but really, I didn't see anything recognizable. It is easier to see other traffic at night and it appeared that the sky around us was full of airplanes. So far, this was one of my favorite flights. The view at night is spectacular and generally, the winds are calmer. I spent a lot of time planning for the flight and didn't use any of my calculations. I didn't record any checkpoints or do any of the calculations. I've got to work on that!

Saturday, March 28, 1998 Total Hours: 40.6

Training was canceled due to high winds. Winds were from 200 degrees at 24 knots gusting to 40 knots. Nobody should fly in this!

Sunday, March 29, 1998 Total Hours: 41.6

Ah, a beautiful day. There's no wind and the sky is clear. We practiced a normal takeoff and landing, a short field takeoff and landing and a soft-short field takeoff and landing. My landings were pretty good even though my patterns were only fair. The first pattern was wide and long on final and I had to use power to maintain the glide. but the touchdowns were very good. I looked farther ahead and concentrated on maintaining the center line. I had active rudder and ailerons until touchdown. Pretty good. Bill demonstrated a short field takeoff and landing for me. My landings were just as good.

After the airplane was towed to the hangar, I noticed that the nose wheel strut had collapsed. Bill reported it and said it would be checked out. I asked Bill if he thought I caused it and he said that all my landings were good. I had put no undue stress on the nose wheel. Got a '1' for the day! I could do the cross country on a day like today, it was so perfect. I'm anxious to get a solo cross country behind me.

Tuesday, March 31, 1998 Total Hours: 43.0

I went out to the airport about 5:30 P.M. and did the preflight. 97Y had a new strut put on the front and no one had flown it since my last flight. The temperature was about 78 and the humidity was high. This made the density altitude higher and we could really tell the difference on climb out. There is definitely a performance degradation in these conditions. I wonder what it will be like when it gets really hot!

We did power-off and power-on stalls. I didn't recover fast enough. I guess I was waiting for the full stall, not just an imminent stall. I did steep turns, better than before but I still need practice to perfect them. I gained and lost altitude. Next, we headed back and did 4 landings. By the time we got back it was dark so I was able to count the landings as night. This completed the night requirement.

All of the landings were passable but Bill ragged me about details like flaring at the precise time, soft touchdown and maintaining the centerline. It was good practice and I certainly got more comfortable and confident. We had 1.4 hours and, overall, it was a good night. Bill gave me a grade of 1.5 because my stalls and steep turns need precision.

Saturday, April 4, 1998 Total Hours: 43.0

Training was canceled due to low ceilings and high winds. I bought a Cessna 172P Pilot Operating Handbook (which is much more informative than the flimsy little pamphlet that came with 97Y).

Thanks to Bill's constant reminders, I'm starting to notice the subtle details of flying. My night cross country experience taught me that flying at night, even a clear night, requires much more reliance on instruments than daytime VFR flight. It's easy to get lost in the beauty of the twinkling lights on a clear crisp night. I also learned more about density altitude and how it affects the performance of the aircraft. I learned more about the operations at a tower controlled airport as well. Although the weather delays were disappointing, I learned valuable lessons about weather conditions and about making the go/no-go decision on my own. I'm starting to spread my wings!

Solo Cross Country

It was time to put my training to the test. A solo cross country flight brings together all the aircraft control skills, navigation training and ability to survive in the flight environment. For the first time I began to feel like a real pilot.

Sunday, April 5, 1998 Total Hours: 44.8

I did it! My first solo cross country flight to Ashtabula Co. and back! I was scared to death and very nervous. I had been nervous since last Tuesday because I knew it was coming and it looked like the weather would be clear. Yesterday was clear too, but very windy. Although I scheduled at 8:00, 10:00 and then noon, I finally gave up. I was really, really hoping to get some crosswind experience before this trip, but it was not to be. I got the weather on Sunday morning and it was predicted to be very clear with winds from the NNW at 12 knots. That's not too bad for runway 01 at Kent but it is a direct crosswind at Ashtabula Co. (7G2). That had me worried. I was signed off for 7 knot crosswind on my solo endorsement. Bill signed me off for 10 knot crosswind for this trip. He had faith!

I preflighted on the ramp and to me the wind was howling! It probably wasn't that bad but my imagination was going wild. My preflight check detected that the oil was below 6 quarts and the book says it should be no less than 6. I checked everything else and walked back to the office to get the oil. After adding a quart, I walked back just as Bill was coming out to remind me to get my flight plan for filing. So, I walked all the way back to the plane and got my bag, duh! I went back to the office and Bill signed me off. I called flight services and filed my flight plan and rechecked the weather. No surprises. They told me the winds could be light or heavy from the NNW. Erie, PA reported winds from 330 degrees at 14 knots gusting to 20 knots which didn't help my apprehension. That was only 30 miles from where I was going. Akron predicted 320 degrees at 9 knots with light to gusting winds. So what was it? Bill checked out the airplane and shook my hand and said "Good luck, see you later, don't forget to close your flight plan."

OK, I'm alone in the cockpit, where do I start? Oh yes, that's what checklists are for. I set my radios for Kent, Ashtabula Co. and the Cleveland Flight Service Station (FSS). I set the Jefferson VOR on the Nav radio, OBS set to 045, and for added help, I set the LORAN to 7G2. I nervously got through the start up procedure and began to taxi to runway 01. I remembered to set the directional gyro (DG) on the way down. Man, is the wind at 40 knots? I had a death grip on the yoke to keep the ailerons from flapping off. Oh, they just said 10 knots. I performed the runup, looked around, taxied out, and departed runway 01. I was on my way.

Once off the ground there was no turning back. This is the same feeling I had on my first solo. Of course, I wasn't as experienced then and didn't know any better. Also, there was absolutely no wind then. Not so today. Takeoff came earlier than expected partly because I was minus 220 pounds of instructor and heading into a strong wind. No problem on takeoff. The climb was bumpy but manageable and I was headed for 3,500 feet.

I had my first checkpoint, I-80, in sight ahead of me. I called Cleveland Flight Services to open my flight plan (I never did this before). No problem there. I opened it successfully at 1:26 local time. My estimated time enroute was filed for 40 minutes which turned out to be perfect. I logged the first checkpoint, checked my heading and read the engine gauges. Everything was normal except the air was a little choppy. I was at 4000 feet before I knew it. Oops. I descended to

3500 and tried to hold it. The next checkpoint, Highway 422 was in sight and it looked like I was on course. There is a huge lake with highway 422 crossing over a bridge which was easy to see. I was exactly on course as I flew over a tower to the east of the bridge. The next interim checkpoint was Geauga Co. airport, which I had designated as my alternate airport in case of emergency. I never saw it! I must have flown right over it, but all the fields looked the same. I crossed over Highway 322 a little uncertain that it was the right road, but it matched the map and I logged it. Up ahead, I could see Lake Roaming Rock and I was on course for the northwest tip of it, as planned. I could clearly see Cleveland and Lake Erie. By this time I had calmed down a bit but I knew I was getting closer to landing. The LORAN told me I was about 17 miles from Ashtabula so I switched to their frequency. I swear, there must have been a dozen airplanes in various parts of the traffic pattern. You'd have thought it was O'Hare International in Chicago! As I logged the checkpoint at the lake, I spotted what looked like the airport about 10 miles away. Yep, it was the town of Jefferson. The VOR needle moved as I pass the station and I started my descent to 1900 feet. I called Unicom and got no response. I tried again as I got closer and got the airport advisory. The active runway was 26 as I expected. The winds were NNW at 10 knots. OK, that was the scoop.

I entered the pattern after doing my GUMPS check and remembered all the steps including radio calls. When I turned to base, I was extremely high. The wind must have held me up when I turned into it. I thought for a moment that I might be able to get the plane down, but when I got to about 300 feet, I thought better of it and did a go-around. Go full throttle, establish a climb, retract the flaps and announce what I'm doing. In the climb, I realized I'd forgotten to turn the carb heat off, so I did and climbed back out to pattern altitude. I set it all up again with a little wider pattern this time and descended the way I should. Airspeed good, glide angle good, crabbed to the right, lined up with center line. Everything looked good. I knew what I had to do with the rudder to get aligned with the runway and did a little test before I crossed the threshold. OK, round out, rudder, aileron to the wind. Oops, not enough! I was aligned with the runway all right, but drifted left because of the wind. Thank God its a wide runway. I got the aileron in but it wasn't enough to get back to the center line. I landed straight but left of the stripe. I did it!

I taxied to the ramp like I knew what I was doing. Once parked, I shut down and gave a tremendous sigh of relief. Wow! I was within 3 minutes of my planned flight time. If I hadn't done a go-around it would have been right on!

I locked the aircraft and went inside the terminal. I called Flight Services to close the flight plan, drank a can of lemonade, read the bulletin board, had the attendant at the desk sign my log book and checked the weather terminal. I relaxed for a minute, watching a Pink Panther movie on the TV, reviewed my flight plan for the return and mustered up the courage to go out and do it again! I did a thorough preflight and called for a radio check and airport advisory and got no answer (asleep at the switch) and so I taxied back to Runway 26 after checking the wind sock (standing straight out, must be 50 knots!). I did my runup checks and waited for an inbound airplane to do a touch and go.

I taxied out for another adventure. Radios set, LORAN set for 1G3 (Kent State), engine looked good. I was off again. Aileron into the wind, again I reached takeoff speed faster than I expected and was drifting left. I firmly applied elevator pressure and left the ground drifting to the left. I lowered the nose a bit to pick up speed and crabbed into the wind. I was off! I looked back at about 500 feet and was tracking right of the runway, a little too much correction. Oh, well. I climbed to pattern altitude and turned to my heading. Over Jefferson, I called Cleveland radio to open the flight plan and could not contact them. At 3000 feet I leveled off and headed for the tip of Lake Roaming Rock, on course. I finally got Cleveland to respond and took care of the flight plan. I was off at 3:01 P.M..

The return flight was bumpy. I found all my checkpoints (still didn't see my alternate site, Geauga County Airport) and before long, I could see Kent State. I was still 15 miles away. I located my last checkpoint and descended. Near the Terex plant, I turned toward the airport and announced I was on a 45 for downwind runway 01. The airport advisory said the wind was NNW at 10. Another airplane was also entering the pattern. I radioed to let him know that I had him in sight. He told me that he would circle and follow me in. Thank you! I got in the pattern in great shape and descended normally. I was crabbed to the left on final and once again, rudder was good for alignment, but I allowed too much drift and drifted off to the right. I also kept a little too much power as I crossed the runway threshold, but it wasn't too bad. I rolled out and missed the turnoff. I heard the airplane behind me call a go-around because I was still on the runway. Sorry! I taxied to the end, pulled off the runway and did the post flight checklist (I even remembered to turn the landing light on, both times!). After another huge sigh of relief, I taxied to the fuel pump. I saw Bill walking out to greet me.

What a cool trip! I told Bill about it and that I feel like I really accomplished something. I guess compared to Lindbergh, this was nothing, but to me it was a major milestone. I went in and closed my flight plan. I estimated that I would use 11 gallons of fuel and it was actually 12.4. My time coming home was 7 minutes longer than I had planned. Not too bad. Grin, grin, grin! I felt really good about what I had done and felt a great relief that it was done!

Bill planned my next cross country for the following weekend and the final one two weeks after that. Then, he said, we'd talk about scheduling the che...che...checkride! Gulp!

Tuesday, April 7, 1998 Total Hours: 45.7

The wind today was from 100 degrees at 8 knots. It was perfect for practicing crosswind landings. Bill and I flew the pattern 5 times and each one was good. After completing the cross country I had gained a great deal of confidence. Tonight added to my confidence. The patterns were very good, just the right amount of crab. The turn to final was good except for one wide turn. Each landing was increasingly better but the last one was a squeaker.

I hope I'm not too overconfident. I guess I need to practice maneuvers again. They can be humbling. I'm also able to verbalize what I'm doing so Bill knows I'm in control. It feels good. I hope the weather is good for Thursday so I can get another practice in before the next cross country on Saturday.

Thursday, April 9, 1998 Total Hours: 45.7

The lesson was canceled due to weather. There were thunderstorms and tornadoes in the area.

The solo cross country flight to Ashtabula was a real boost to my confidence. I'd learned a lot about the flight environment and handling the airplane was becoming much more natural. I felt proud that I've been able to fly an airplane to an airport over 50 miles away and lived to tell about it! That was an accomplishment not everyone has experienced. I knew that I had a lot to learn but I'd made it this far.

I still had this annoying voice in my head telling me that something could go wrong. However, I'm much more confident that I can handle unexpected events. As I thought about it, the go-around that I did at Ashtabula was an example of good judgment. With less experience and training, I might have tried to land in an uncomfortable and potentially dangerous situation. It could have had a very bad result. I know that I made the right decision and that helps me convince myself that I'm really starting to understand.

I also learned that things don't always go as planned. You must be prepared for the unexpected, anticipate what will happen and adapt to the current conditions. Kind of like life.

The Medium Cross Country

My medium cross country flight involved landing at three airports at least 50 miles apart. This trip required me to land at a tower controlled airport that was bigger and busier than the ones I was used to. That was a scary thought. I remember the questions that went through my mind. Would I remember what to say? Would I understand the instructions given by the controller? They seem to speak in a rapid, foreign tongue over a bad radio crackling with static. Would the controllers and pilots be laughing at me for sounding so stupid? Would they be able to tell that I was a rookie?

I told myself, "So what? Just do as you were taught and pay close attention. If you don't understand, ask. Be confident in what you've learned and plan ahead." I had a week to think about this flight and I had scripted out every radio frequency change, every checkpoint and everything to say. I felt a little over prepared, but it made me feel better. Whatever works.

Saturday, April 11, 1998 Total Hours: 48.4

What an awesome solo cross country flight to Sandusky and Mansfield and back! I had excellent flying weather. The skies were clear with light winds. A great day! I was nervous but not quite as much as the first trip. I preflighted, checked the weather and filed my flight plan, while Bill checked my work and signed me off. I took off on runway 19 for Sandusky.

I headed southwest until I intercepted the Akron VOR, then headed west. I tried to open my flight plan but the radio traffic was so heavy I never heard them respond to me. I found all my checkpoints and had a smooth ride to Sandusky, a small town on the shores of Lake Erie. When I got there, I called for an airport advisory, got in the traffic pattern and landed on runway 27. It was very interesting to approach over water to the end of the runway. I didn't want to be short on this one! I made a good glide with the right airspeed and touched down straight and soft. Excellent! The airport was a little strange since there was only one exit in the middle of the field. I taxied all the way to the end, waited for an airplane to depart and then back-taxied to the mid-field exit. I pulled up at the pump and the lineman topped off the fuel tanks. I went in and paid, got my log book signed, closed my flight plan and got the weather briefing in the "pilot lounge", a small room off the restaurant.

As luck would have it, Jim, my first CFI, was just coming in with a student and we chatted for a minute. It was good to see him again.

Starting the next leg of my flight, I did an abbreviated preflight and taxied out after setting the radios. Next was the tough part, flying into controlled airspace with controllers, radar and everything! I got the ATIS, opened my flight plan (using the VOR frequency to receive) and headed south. I saw all my checkpoints and maintained heading and altitude.

I called Mansfield approach, and told them that I was a student pilot. They had me squawk 0333 on the transponder to identify me on radar. Once identified, they told me to set up for right traffic for runway 23. When they handed me off to the tower, they changed me over to runway 32, right traffic. I was on downwind for 32 when they asked me if I had traffic on final in sight. Negative contact (this means 'no'). I was asked to advise them when I had traffic in sight. I located the inbound airplane, reported that I had it in sight and was cleared to land on runway 32. I turned base and final and set up a good landing on the centerline. What a wide runway! It always amazes me how much concrete there is at a larger airport. I taxied off and they directed me to the parking area.

I went into the terminal and closed my flight plan. I didn't know where to go to re-fuel and then I remembered that I should have asked for directions to Richland Aviation. I started 97Y and asked the controller for directions to Richland. Once there, I re-fueled from a truck, paid for it, had my book signed and started up again. I called Mansfield ground for clearance to taxi to the runway and proceeded to runway 32. I did the runup in a hurry because there was a small jet behind me. I was cleared for takeoff and a right turn to the east was approved, and was off! That was pretty easy! About 10 miles out, VFR was approved. Good day to you!

I flew directly over Ashland which was south of my course, so turned to the north and got on course. Again, I saw all my checkpoints and headed for Kent State. It was beginning to get a little bumpy, but not too bad. I could see Akron-Canton, Akron-Fulton and Kent State airports from several miles away. I called Kent and got the active runway, which was 01. I got on the 45 for downwind and flew a good pattern, but was fast. I landed it OK, but again the wind drifted me off to the right of centerline. Just like last time but not quite as bad. It was an OK landing and the other two were very good, so all in all a good flying experience!

I pulled up to the pump 45 minutes later than I expected and there was another student waiting for the airplane. He didn't seem to mind too much about the wait. I compared my plans to the actual results and they were pretty close in time and fuel used. I spent more time on the ground than expected and my ground speed was less than I calculated. I closed my flight plan, settled the bill and wished everyone a happy Easter. Success! Another boost in confidence!

Tuesday, April 14, 1998 Total Hours: 48.4

Training was canceled due to weather. Heavy rain.

Thursday, April 16, 1998 Total Hours: 49.4

The weather was threatening all day but I was able fly with Bill anyway. The winds were predicted to be 250 degrees at 13 gusting to 18 with storms predicted for later. Near the airport it was actually clearing and the winds were less than 10 knots. We practiced pattern work. Five times around with short field, soft field and normal takeoffs and landings. I thought the landings were good although I dropped a couple in hard. The winds were very erratic above the tree line and just before crossing the threshold. I thought I handled it all very well and Bill gave me an 'excellent' grade for the day.

Saturday, April 18, 1998 Total Hours: 50.6

Another nice day. We practiced slow flight, power-off and power-on stalls, emergency descent, S-Turns and reviewed other emergency procedures. We also did short field and soft field takeoffs and landings. Bill gave me another 'excellent' for the day. Both landings were on the center line, one was a little long and the other I kind of dropped in, but both were acceptable. We also performed a go-around which I did pretty well.

After landing, we talked about the upcoming schedule and the...the...the...(gulp) checkride! We went down and met Tom, the examiner, and scheduled my practical test for May 16. Bill said the oral exam might take an hour and half and the flight about 45 minutes. Tom told me to study the Practical Test Standards (PTS) and call him that week to get instructions for planning a cross country trip. His fee would be $125.

Once on the test schedule, Bill and I did some advanced planning to get me ready for the checkride. We planned some instrument work, a flight with Mike (the chief instructor) in N62953, the long solo cross country, solo maneuvers practice, a stage check with Mike and an extended briefing with Bill to review the upcoming checkride. Finally, I could see the end of this phase of my training!

Thursday, April 23, 1998 Total Hours: 51.9

Cool! Another new experience. We took off runway 01 into a cross-wind and headed to the practice area. I was wearing the 'foggles' for the first time. Foggles are special frosted glasses that are worn to allow the student to see the instrument panel but not look out the windows. As we approached the practice area, Bill told me to put them on. I could clearly see the instruments and if I tried, I could see a little out the side window and over the cowling. I tried to not look in order to get the most from this lesson.

We did straight and level, slow flight, approach to landing stalls, several constant rate turns to heading and climbs and descents at various speeds and attitudes. It was easier than I expected but I was sure it would get tiring after a while. Bill told me to close my eyes and put my head down while he put us in an "unusual attitude." This was very strange.

Attitude refers to the position of the airplane like nose-up, nose-down, bank left or right. The drill requires the instructor to maneuver the airplane in such a way that the student loses track of which direction is up. The object of the drill is to read the instruments to recover from a situation where outside visual references are lost, such as inadvertently flying into a cloud. Bill turned and climbed and turned and slowed and speeded up several times to confuse me. It amazed me how quickly my senses betrayed me. I wasn't sure if we were going up or down. When he said recover, we were diving with a right bank. I leveled out using instruments only and maintained altitude with no problems. That was weird! The lesson here is trust my instruments, not my senses.

I removed the foggles and we did S-turns then headed back. I entered the pattern on a 45 for upwind, crossed at the numbers and turned downwind for landing. I came in too fast because the wind was pushing the airplane and consequently I couldn't slow down to 70 knots before I was well past the base turning point. I was also too close on downwind which made a tight downwind-base-final turn. I landed, but it wasn't pretty. Next time around was near perfect. I held a little power, like on a soft field landing, until settling to touchdown and barely squeaked the tires. Bill was impressed and said that was perfect! He asked, "Want to try again or quit on a perfect landing?" I said, "Let's do it again." "OK," he said, "but your last one has to be better and that will be hard to beat." I went around again and my last landing was perfect. A slight crosswind, soft touchdown on the left wheel then the right and barely a peep from the tires. This was fun!

Looking back, the medium cross country flight was the turning point in my training. I began to put all the pieces together. I had proven to myself that I could navigate and control the airplane. I worked to hone my skills and became more precise. The peaks and valleys between confidence and no confidence are smaller now. I guess this training program which seemed, at times, to be haphazard, really does work.

THE LONG CROSS COUNTRY

With the checkride less than a month away, I turned my focus on getting the last requirements out of the way including, the long cross country flight. This one requires 100 mile legs and two tower controlled airports in fairly busy places.

Saturday, April 25, 1998 Total Hours: 56.2

Man, am I tired. Today was the long solo cross country flight from Kent State to Toledo to Ohio State to Kent State. Three hundred and six nautical miles with a three hour and thirty-nine minute flight time. A total Hobbs time of 4.3 hours. It was another perfect day for a cross country. There was little or no wind with a temperature of about 60 degrees.

I flew to Toledo at 2500 feet to stay under the Cleveland Class B airspace. I found every checkpoint on this leg. Landmarks were easy to find and I was never in doubt about my position. I tracked the Akron VOR outbound and Waterville VOR inbound to Toledo. I had no problems with the radio or the Class C airspace! At larger airports, wide runways are easy to spot. I must have been ten to twelve miles away when I spotted it. I landed at Toledo on runway 16 and was a little high and consequently fast, but I pulled off a passable landing on the center line. I gassed up at TOL Aviation, closed my flight plan, checked the weather with the briefer and took off for Ohio State. I had left Kent State (1G3) at 9:06 A.M. and arrived in Toledo at 10:32 A.M. Total time to Toledo was one hour and twenty-six minutes.

The second leg to Ohio State started at 11:18 A.M. and ended at 12:28 P.M.. Ninety-three nautical miles in one hour and ten minutes. I followed the Waterville VOR outbound. The controller indicated that he would watch me for another 20 miles and I agreed. I never heard him terminate radar services so I switched to Columbus approach when the time came. I was able to identify all my checkpoints even though I was a little left of course. The wind was from the west and was blowing me off course so I had to constantly correct. I also had trouble contacting Columbus approach because of all the radio traffic. Finally, the controller acknowledged me and had me switch over immediately to the OSU tower. The tower instructed me to fly left downwind for 27L (runway 27 Left) and watch for inbound traffic on final. I never saw the other traffic. I think it was already past me. Finally, the tower cleared me to turn base and to land. It was a sweet landing. I taxied to the FBO (fixed based operation), fueled up and got my log book signed.

I was supposed to have the airplane back by 2:00 P.M. so I didn't spend much time on the ground. I called ground control and the controller mildly chastised me for forgetting to tell him who, what, when, where, etc. I gave him the information and was cleared to taxi to 27L for departure. After the runup, I called tower and was cleared for takeoff. Once in the air, I was cleared to turn on course. I found the first checkpoint and then struggled somewhat to stay on course. I made good time because the wind was behind me but had some difficulty finding the checkpoints. I saw all but one and for each one, I had to correct my course. It was a good thing the LORAN worked for navigation, although, I could have navigated without it. About 15 miles out, I spotted the familiar landmarks of Akron. I started my descent and called Kent State Unicom. There was a lot of local traffic here. I got in the pattern and landed long. I suppose I'm not used to the feel of landing with just one person on board. I was high but pulled it out nicely.

After I got home, I compared my planned times and estimated fuel to the actual values. I was actually pretty close, but I'll have to improve. I would rather over estimate the fuel required than under estimate.

Overall, it was a great trip. I had clear skies most of the way, with a little haze on the last leg. Almost no wind made it fun to land since I didn't have to worry about using my crosswind skills. I learned more about the radio and what problems can be encountered when you can't get a word in edgewise. I had trouble opening the flight plan for the last leg and finally looked up the frequency at Mansfield and got through. On a busy day, there is a lot of radio traffic, so it's good to be brief and clear. I seemed to be rushed near the airports, but I handled it all right.

That was a long trip. I gained experience at tower controlled airports and in navigation. The longer legs were enjoyable since there was more time to enjoy the scenery and sunshine. I also realized that I wasn't gripping the yoke as hard. Those first few solo flights were white-knucklers. I guess I'm starting to relax and really enjoy it. I felt really good to have this one behind me. Now I could focus on getting ready for the checkride. The pressure was on!

CHECKRIDE PREPARATION

With the cross country flights out of the way, it was time to buckle down and focus on preparing for the checkride. By now, I've experienced almost all the things I need to know and do for the practical test. It was time to practice, practice, practice.

Tuesday, April 28, 1998 Total Hours: 57.8

I wasn't prepared for this one, but it was a great lesson. I flew with Mike because Bill was not available. Mike said we would simulate a cross country and he asked me to plan a flight to Youngstown. I took a few minutes and mapped it out, got the winds and made the calculations. We went out and preflighted N62953. I took longer than normal on the preflight, explaining to Mike what I was doing. It looked good so we pulled it out of the hangar and taxied out to runway 01. There was very little surface wind.

We departed to the east, picked up my first checkpoint and climbed to 3500 feet. After the first checkpoint, we diverted to Cuyahoga County airport. I turned north then set up for a VOR tracking to Chardon. We discussed how I would determine the distance and time and how I would amend my flight plan in route with the Flight Service Station (FSS). After that we headed back in the general direction of Portage County. After a couple of clearing turns, I did slow flight, power-off and power-on stalls. I thought I did these pretty well. Next we approached Portage County to practice landings. I overflew the field to get a look at the windsock and determined that I would use runway 27. The wind aloft was blowing from the north. I set up in the pattern and did a lousy approach followed by a lousy soft field landing. I was high and hot. I couldn't seem to make this airplane descend in a stable way. I did land without danger, but it wasn't good. Next we did a soft field takeoff and headed back.

On the way back, we did a simulated emergency approach to landing. Mike taught me a lesson on entering the pattern. When entering on crosswind, the pilot should fly over mid-field or over the numbers. I had crossed the runway path a couple of miles away from the departure end. Mike explained that I was almost exactly where a departing aircraft would be. Crossing mid-field or over the numbers ensures that the airplane is out of the path of departing traffic. He said I was a good pilot and just need more time to get the judgment down. Overall, it was one of the most informative and constructive lessons I've had and I was tired when it was done. I had logged 1.6 hours and it was nearly dark when we arrived at KSU. A little humbling. I would have been more comfortable in 97Y but this was a really good experience for me. I've grown to appreciate Mike's style. He's a really good instructor who gives you your money's worth with every lesson.

Thursday, April 30, 1998 Total Hours: 57.8

Bill and I went out to the hangar and preflighted. Just as we were about to pull the airplane out, it started to rain. Good preflight practice. Canceled due to weather.

Tuesday, May 5, 1998 Total Hours: 59.6

What an adventure! I was nervous about this one because it was the first real solo where I needed to perform the maneuvers without someone sitting next to me. The weather was fine and no wind at all. I completed the preflight and Bill and I pulled the airplane out. He left to meet with another student and I was on my own.

I did all the necessary pre-takeoff checklist items and talked myself through everything. I liked the sound of my own voice on the intercom. It was reassuring. I smoothly took off from runway 19 and climbed to 2000 feet then headed east over Kent and Ravenna to the practice area. I had scripted out all that I wanted to accomplish if I had time. First I climbed to 3,300 feet and carefully watched for traffic. I did clearing turns and then steep turns. They weren't too bad. I held altitude by adding a little power, remembered to take the power out when I leveled off and went into the steep turn in the other direction. Good. Next on the agenda was slow flight. I slowed down more quickly than normal and the stall warning indicator went off several times. No real stall, just a warning. I hung in the air a while and did 90 degree heading changes with no problem. I really do know what I'm doing! Next the stall. For no good reason, I was apprehensive about this maneuver. I pulled back on the yoke until the nose pitched down in a stall, added power, carb heat off and retracted the flaps in increments, just like I was taught. I didn't do a great job holding the heading, but then I was a little nervous. I slowed to about 65 knots and added full power, pitched up and did a power-on stall. It felt like I was going straight up and that I might start sliding backwards. I did fine! So fine, in fact, that I continued with my script and did the whole sequence again after a few clearing turns. I saw three C-130's in the distance, but not close enough to bother me.

I checked the clock and had plenty of time to do more. So, on with the script. I descended to 2000 feet over the arsenal and did two turns around a water tower, rectangular course (not much wind), and S-turns until I ran out of road.

I turned west to return to the airport. The sun was in my eyes and it was a little hazy. I perceived that there were sun rays coming through a few clouds to the west and then I thought I saw a rain shower to the north. Sure enough, as I flew over Kent to get in the pattern, I saw rain to the north and it was heading in my direction. I thought I had time so I proceeded. I called downwind and then base for 19 when I got a report from the Unicom operator. "Aircraft in the pattern, be advised that we just had a lightning strike on the ramp". Gulp! I acknowledged that and said that I was going around. I headed west and south and made a decision to get out of the air. I clearly saw the blimp hangar at Akron-Fulton airport and decided that things looked a whole lot better there! I got out my Terminal chart, found the radio frequency and executed a near perfect landing on runway 25 at Akron-Fulton!

I parked at the Airspect Aviation ramp and went to the pay phone. I called Commercial Aviation, got the answering machine, and left a message. I figured they would be worried about me by now. Next, I called the Kent State Airport office. I asked them to get a message to Bill that I was safely on the ground. I gave the number of the pay phone and went back to the airplane to wait. I was straightening up the cockpit when I realized that the phone was ringing. I sprinted the 50 yards to answer it and heard Bill at the other end. He was glad I was safely down and he said that what I did was a very smart thing. He would sign me off for good judgment, decision making and for diversion in flight! He checked the weather and I suggested that he go to the airport office and look at radar. He did and called me back. It still didn't look too good. He said he'd watch it for 15 minutes and call me back. He called and said, "Looks like it's off to the east. I think you can make it if you come up Route 8 west of the airport." OK, I'd do it!

By then, the sun was almost down and darkness was falling (pretty dramatic, eh?). I couldn't get anyone to talk to me on the radio at Akron-Fulton so I checked the wind sock, scanned for traffic and departed on runway 25. I flew north at about 2300 feet to stay out of Akron/Canton airspace and called Kent at about 5 miles out. They were now using runway 01. Good, it's easier to enter the pattern for 01 from the west. I entered the pattern and tried to get the runway lights to come on. They wouldn't work! It was still dusk and I could see well enough. I landed without problem and Bill called me as I rolled out on the runway. "97Y just taxi on back to the hangar, the fuel pumps are not working now" and then, "Welcome home, Bob"!

Thursday, May 7, 1998 Total Hours: 59.6

I canceled the flight lesson due to bad weather. The radar indicated rain off to the west and moving our way. Instead of flying, we did ground work in preparation for the checkride. We reviewed aircraft records and then Bill grilled me with questions. He asked me to prepare a flight plan for a trip to Toledo Metcalf airport using today's weather. We talked about various subjects in an unorganized way. Bill reminded me that the checkride will consist of about an hour and a half of oral questions and a 45 minute flight. We'd see.

Saturday, May 9, 1998 Total Hours: 60.8

I flew with Mike today on a 'stage check'. This is done so that a different instructor can evaluate your progress. I explained the preflight to Mike as I did it and then we taxied out to runway 01 for departure. Following the runup we did a normal takeoff and as we climbed, we reached a scattered cloud layer. We did slow flight with turns, ascent and descent, power-off stall, then we descended to around 2000 feet and did turns around a point, S-turns and then some instrument work on the way back to the airport. I put the foggles on and Mike navigated us back into the pattern, crosswind over the numbers, downwind, carb heat on, reduce power, descend, flaps, turn to base and final and then he let me take off the foggles! That was strange! I did a normal landing with a slight crosswind. Next I did a soft field takeoff, soft field landing, short field takeoff, short field landing which ended in a go-around because I was long, and then I did a really good short field landing.

Once inside I asked Mike if he thought I was ready. His hesitation told me that he wasn't sure. We reviewed the lesson and Mike gave me some pointers. He then said that only I can tell if I'm ready and that everything that I did today was within the standards required. I didn't get a great feeling of confidence from this, but it was OK. Bill gave me the Practical Test application form to fill out (one to practice and a real one.)

I still need 1.6 hours of instrument time before I'm really qualified. If I get rained out one day next week, I may not be ready. Come on weather! I also scheduled another flight with Mike at noon next Friday, just in case.

Tuesday, May 12, 1998 Total Hours: 62.1

I've been a nervous wreck for the last few days thinking about the checkride. There isn't enough time in the day for all the studying I want to do. I'm fairly confident about the oral and still shaky about the flying. I want it to be perfect and I want to remember everything.

Today, I arrived at the airport a little early and Bill wasn't there yet. I sat outside waiting for him to return with the airplane. He landed with another student and taxied past the pumps back to the hangar. I met them there and found that the plane's left magneto was acting up. I went back to the office and told Al about it and he'd check it out. He also asked me if any other airplanes were available. I checked and found that N62953 was available. Bill gave me his keys and I went to hangar 13, but the plane wasn't there. I found it in line at the pumps waiting to be fueled and relieved the other student who was waiting for the fueling to be done.

I preflighted at the pump and soon Bill came out and we were on our way. I needed 1.6 hours of instrument time so that's what we planned to do. I departed on 19, climbed to 2500 feet and ran into condensation, so we descended to 2000 feet. I put the foggles on and we followed the Jefferson VOR all the way to Ashtabula county and back and I didn't take the foggles off until we were in the pattern back at Kent State.

I landed just fine, not high like I did the last time I flew this airplane. It was actually kind of boring to stare at the instruments. I maintained heading and altitude fine and made all the turns that Bill asked for. We did a climb and descent with no problem. Bill said that I would make a very good instrument student.

I got 1.3 instrument hours on this flight and we'd get the rest on Thursday. I also need to practice flapless landings. I called Tom, the examiner, yesterday and he gave me the destination of my cross country plan—Sidney, OH, near Dayton. I asked him about the schedule since I have the airplane from 9:00 A.M. to noon and someone else has it after me. He said we should probably start earlier, so we agreed to start at 7:00 A.M. Saturday. I asked him who to make the check out to and how much he weighs so I could calculate the weight and balance. He said call anytime if I have more questions. Just a few more days.

I have found that I get nervous thinking about flying, but once I get in the airplane, it goes away. Hope that's true on the checkride.

Thursday, May 14, 1998 Total Hours: 63.0

This was a dual flight with Bill. Nice warm day and hazy at 2500 feet. We departed runway 19 and climbed up to 2500 feet. I put the foggles on and we did turns to heading, climb, descent and pretty soon I had completed the instrument requirement.

We flew to the north practice area around Geauga Lake and Twinsburg. I was familiar with this area, since I work there. We did steep turns, slow flight, power-off and power-on stalls, emergency descent, S-turns and then headed back down Rt. 91. We got in the pattern for runway 01 since the wind was out of the north and no one was in the pattern. Bill demonstrated a slip to landing and then I did one. That wasn't too bad. I did fine on mine. We took off one more time and I did a short soft field landing. That, too, was good.

We put the aircraft up and went in to sign me off! Bill signed my logbook and the application form indicating that he thought I was ready. We went over a few things and Bill told me not to worry, I'd do fine. I told him that I get very nervous just thinking about the test but then, when I fly, my confidence immediately comes back. I hope that holds true during the checkride.

It's hard to describe the mental torture that I've put myself through getting ready. I can do this as long as I don't go brain dead from nerves. I have to finish my flight plan tonight and I'm taking tomorrow off so I can study, fly with Mike at noon, review the aircraft logs, sit in the airplane and imagine what will happen, study some more and get some sleep (right!) I can't wait for this part to be over.

Friday, May 15, 1998 Total Hours: 63.5

I scheduled another flight with Mike just to get one more in before the test. Since I had taken the day off to prepare, I scheduled to fly at noon. We had a little trouble with the left magneto (the same one that acted up Tuesday) so Mike showed me how to lean it and run it up at higher rpm to burn out any carbon deposits.

We departed and did steep turns, S-turns and landings. I could not keep the steep turns at altitude. We did four or five before I began to get it right. Airspeed was all over the place and it wasn't much of a confidence builder. I did passable S-turns and excellent landings. We did short field and soft field landings and they were both very good. Now I have a fear of failing steep turns. I should have stayed home! Oh well, more experience is good and hopefully I've got that out of my system.

I went home for lunch and then back to the airport. I got the airplane maintenance records and reviewed them carefully marking each significant log entry like the last annual inspection, altimeter, static pressure system, transponder and Emergency Locator Transmitter (ELT) tests. Mike let me take the records with me so I'd have them in the morning. I asked Mike for windshield cleaner since it was buggy. He gave me some in the office but then later said that he'd asked that the airplane be washed for me. I went down to the hangar and got the Pilot's Operating Handbook (POH) and other documents to review. Meanwhile a young man was cleaning the airplane. I reviewed the books and after the guy left, I got in the airplane. Still buggy! I spent a few minutes in the cockpit just going through in my mind what the flight test would be like.

After that, I went home and hit the books. I studied until about 11:00 P.M.. I also completed my flight plan and checked the weather forecast. It didn't look as perfect as I had imagined. There was a cold front moving this way with rain, thundershowers and higher winds. I didn't like the looks of it. It was only a 40% chance of rain in the early afternoon and otherwise, VFR conditions. Winds aloft were 210 at 19 knots. I thought I was as ready as I'd ever be so I went to bed. It was hot and sticky and of course the kids were up late. I didn't sleep much and I had the alarm set for 5:00 A.M.

The tension was mounting now. I had completed all the requirements and Bill had endorsed my logbook. I was technically ready. Mentally, I think I was in pretty good shape. It's just a matter of hours now. I was very careful not to tell too many people that I was about to take this test. I guess I didn't want to explain to them if it didn't go well. I had all the book work and flight training behind me now. All that's left is to convince the examiner that I am a competent pilot. I wondered what it would be like.

CHECKRIDE!

I've watched the King video on the Private Pilot Checkride several times. In the video, John King plays the part of a student and an examiner puts him through a very comprehensive oral and flight exam that takes about four hours. I found this to be very informative because it demonstrates a very thorough test. I knew exactly what the examiner must cover. I just didn't know if the examiner would cover a specific topic during the oral exam or during the flight test. I was confident that I'd do well on the oral exam. I also had the same preflight anxiety as always. I just hoped that I'd settle down once in the airplane. I felt like I'd been trained well and I felt like I was ready.

Saturday, May 16, 1998 Total Hours: 63.8

The alarm went off very early for a Saturday. I hopped out of bed and immediately turned on the computer. I made coffee and ate a couple of donuts while I dialed up DUATS to check the weather conditions. There was no real improvement from last night. Still looked to be hazy here with a good chance for rain in the early afternoon. Of course, we would be flying right into the weather so western stations were reporting worse conditions at earlier times. I completed my flight plan with the new information, took a shower and drove to the airport. Akron-Canton was reporting 5 mile visibility and scattered clouds at 25,000 feet. I could tell as I drove to the airport that the visibility wasn't much more than three miles.

I met Bill at 6:50 A.M. and we went to the hangar to get the aircraft documents. I asked Bill if he would take care of cleaning the windshield and do a quick run up to ensure the magnetos would not be a problem. He didn't do either. He said that I could do the runup and, if I had to lean the mixture to clear the magneto, Tom wouldn't mind. He's probably seen that before. OK. I got the papers and notebook with weight and balance information and met Tom, the examiner, in the airport office. He bought me a cup of coffee and we went to the classroom to complete the oral exam.

Tom went through the paperwork first; the application, my medical certificate, my driver's license, test scores and logbook. Tom briefed me on what was going to take place and explained that there are three possible outcomes; pass, fail or discontinued. He explained that, during the flight portion, he is a passenger, I'm the pilot in command. If we have a real emergency, then we'll assist each other. OK, with that, we proceeded with the oral examination.

Tom asked quick questions that did not require complex answers. Answering positively and quickly without a lot of digging through the books probably gave him the feeling that I knew what I was talking about. We covered the following topics (I'm sure I'll think of more later):
- Aircraft maintenance records,
- pilot documentation,
- aircraft documentation,
- privileges of a private pilot,
- medical duration,
- sectional symbols,
- airspace,
- VFR minimums,
- restricted areas,
- MOA,
- military training routes,
- use of oxygen,
- weight and balance and impact of the position of weight,
- flight planning,

- fuel calculation,
- hypoxia,
- hyperventilation,
- drugs,
- alcohol,
- weather reports (METAR, TAF, a little about radar, NOTAMs, PIREPs),
- Airmets,
- Sigmets,
- Convective Sigmets,
- complex and high performance aircraft,
- oil type,
- pitot tube failure,
- static instruments,
- vacuum driven instruments,
- crosswind limits,
- Vx, Vy, Vfe, Vne,
- recency,
- logbook,
- light gun signals,
- spins,
- night flight,
- and lost procedures.

Again, all were very short answer and the whole thing took between 60 and 70 minutes.

There were a few questions that I didn't answer correctly or didn't know and Tom told me the correct answer. They were VOR transmit and receive frequencies, military training routes above and below 1500'(3 digit vs. 4 digit), abandoned railroad symbol, and the difference between high performance and complex aircraft.

"OK," he said, "why don't you go check the weather and we'll get on with the flight portion." I found Bill and he let me in the office. He went down to open the hangar for me and I checked DUATS again. It still didn't look very good west of Mansfield but I didn't expect that we'd go that far anyhow. I called for a weather briefing and really didn't learn anything new. Still marginal for the whole trip. I went down to the hangar and washed the windshield, then I went and got Tom.

He watched me do the preflight and helped me roll the airplane out. Following the checklists, I got the engine started, briefed my passenger, tested the brakes, went through the taxi checklist, and headed out to runway 19 for the runup. During the runup everything worked fine including the magnetos. Whew! I set the radios, cleared the area and taxied out to the runway for departure. We were off!

As I climbed out, it became clear that it was hazier than it looked on the ground. At about 1700 feet, I told Tom that I didn't like the look of it and that I was going to remain in the pattern and land. He agreed with my decision and I turned a little wider than normal on downwind but otherwise made a very good landing. As we touched down, Tom said "Nice landing". I did the after-landing checklist and taxied back to the hangar. What a disappointment. I made the right decision to terminate the flight under the conditions, but now I faced a few more days of agony! Tom said that he liked everything he saw and that I exhibited good piloting. He told me if the maneuvers go like what he has already seen, I'd have no problems passing.

I got credit for the oral, preflight and postflight sections (I, II and XII) of the test and as long as I complete the rest in 60 days, I won't have to retake these parts. I was exhausted from the pressure, studying and lack of sleep. Thankfully, the book part was over and I can concentrate on flying. We scheduled to pick it up again Friday morning at 8:00 A.M. I hoped the weather would be good for this one.

Tuesday, May 19, 1998 Total Hours: 64.9

I scheduled this lesson with Bill to keep my flying skills honed. Not too bad a day. The winds had been gusty but had settled down a bit before 7:00 P.M., the time of my flight lesson. Winds were NNW at 6 knots when we took off. We climbed up to 3000 feet and flew east to the practice area. I performed two sets of steep turns after clearing and they were fine. I rolled into the turns slower, added a little power and looked at the nose on the horizon. I rolled out on the correct heading and into the right turn and did well. OK, I can do this. I also practiced getting into slow flight without losing altitude and it worked fine. We headed back to practice landings.

The wind was stronger now. I got blown in close to the runway on downwind and ended up high and so I did a go-around. The next crosswind landing was dropped in. Oops. It was one of the hardest I've done in a while, but the good news is that I landed straight down the runway in the crosswind. The next time around was as near a perfect crosswind that I think I've ever done. The upwind wheel touched down first and everything! I guess I'm more ready than I thought I was. Let's get it over with!

I figure I'd fly like I was taught and that would be good enough. If it wasn't, then I haven't been taught well enough. Let's go! I asked Al about someone letting me into the hangar on Friday and he gave me my very own personal key in anticipation of my passing the checkride! Not very ceremonious, but it was one of those subtle status symbols. Of course, I didn't know if the key worked or not. I guess I'd find out.

Friday, May 22, 1998 Total Hours: 66.4

The day has finally come! Bill called me last night to tell me that the fuel pumps were broken at Kent State and they couldn't refuel the airplane. If I wanted, I could go to Portage County for fuel or since the plane had only been flown for 1.3 hours after its last refueling, there should be enough fuel for the checkride. Great! Oh yeah, and the landing light was out, but I shouldn't need that. I calculated that there should be enough for the trip without additional fuel. I checked the weather, too. Beautiful! Clear skies, wind 040 at 7 knots. A little more than I hoped for but tolerable.

I preflighted without problem (yes, the key worked) and cleaned the bugs off the windshield. My heart was pounding as I pulled the airplane out of the hangar. I put the hangar door down, got in the airplane and prepared for the flight. I called Kent Unicom and no one answered. Great! I taxied to the pumps and Kent Unicom informed me that the pumps were still not working. OK, I'll just park here for a minute. I shut down and walked over to meet Tom, the designated examiner. We discussed the fuel situation and went over the changes to my flight plan with the new weather information. I told Tom I was more nervous this time than last time since I'd had so long to think about it. Just remember to manage altitude and airspeed, I reminded myself.

We got in and started up, checked the brakes on both sides and taxied down to the runup area for 01. There was a little bit of a crosswind but not strong. During the runup I encountered the old left magneto problem. Too much of a decrease in rpm compared to the right magneto. I leaned and ran up at a higher rpm and that didn't do it. Tom said, "Let me try." He leaned and ran it up even higher for 30 seconds or so. That did it. Whew, we might get off the ground after all. Tom said, "Give me a short field take off", so I put in the 10 degrees of flaps and explained the speeds I would use up to clearing the imaginary 50 foot obstacle. I executed the take off just fine and remembered to retract the flaps. We're off at 8:32 A.M. (and I remembered to write it down)!

At 2000 feet, I announced and turned north west. After clearing the area, I turned south west toward a local tower, leveled off at 2500 feet and simulated opening the flight plan on frequency 122.2. Tom told me earlier that we wouldn't actually open the flight plan. He said if everything was set up right, he would answer my simulated radio call. Tom responded, thankfully. I tuned in the Mansfield VOR before we left and tried to verify the identity of it by listening to the Morse code transmission. I could just barely hear it and the needle was not centered which meant I was probably too far away for it to be useful yet. I noted the time passing my first checkpoint (the tower) and the time was exactly what I had planned. No need to go through all the calculations. We flew to the next checkpoint and I was slightly north about a quarter to half a mile. I noted the time and again, I was right on. Tom leaned the mixture for me.

After passing the checkpoint, Tom diverted us to Wadsworth. Here's where my difficulties began. I checked the map, confirmed that we should be heading south and turned that way. Thinking I knew where we were, I announced that we were 4 miles northeast of the airport and asked for an advisory. No response. I could see the town of Wadsworth out the left window. I simulated the call to Flight Services to cancel my flight plan, since I was not going to continue to Sidney. I flew a while, thinking I knew exactly where I was, but I didn't see the field. I flew south, west, north and then east in a large rectangle and finally spotted the airport. I called again, no answer. I told Tom I would overfly the field and check the wind conditions. On second thought, I'd just get in the pattern for the north east runway and check it out because they probably are landing to the north. I got on a 45 for upwind of the north east runway, crossed over at the numbers and got on downwind for runway 02. Carb heat on, reduce power, 1900 feet, start the descent. I landed fine just past the numbers. It was a good stabilized approach with a little crab and a soft touchdown. I pulled off the runway and tax-ied back to the start of 02.

Tom then asked for a soft field takeoff. Ten degrees of flaps, lift off at 50-55 knots, stay in ground effect, pull the elevator back to keep the nosewheel up. We were off again. No problems. As I climbed out, Tom asked if I had a view limiting device. I told him I have foggles. I started to reach for them and he handed me his taking the controls while I put them on. I re-took the controls and continued climbing. He told me to level off at 2700 feet, which I did. Next we did 180 degree turns to the left and then right using instruments only. This was followed by two unusual attitudes which I handled fine. We finished with the foggles and I took them off.

Next we did steep turns to the left and right. I was a little worried about these since my experience with Mike last week. I focused on the horizon, maintained the altitude within 100 feet and held the bank. No problem. Turn to the right, no problem. Next I did a climbing turn. Good. OK slow flight, another worrisome point. I usually lose altitude on these. This time I did fine and the stall warning indicator came on a couple of times, which, in this situation, is good. It indicated that I was flying at near stall speed. I held right rudder and we did 90 degree turns to the right and then left and then recovered. Next, a power-off stall, which was good. Power-on stall. That was good, too. As I stabilized in cruise, Tom reduced the power to simulate an engine failure. I responded with best glide speed, located a field and headed for it. Tom prompted me "What would you do next?". Checked fuel selector to both, mixture rich, primer in and locked, magnetos on both, carb heat. "OK," Tom said, "go-around." Tom pointed out an intersection and asked me to perform the turn around a point maneuver. Good. Next, Tom asked me to perform S-turns. I did two half circles and that was all.

Tom said, "OK, take me back to Kent." I flew near the Terex building and turned toward Kent State. I called Unicom and found they were still using runway 01. Good! I entered the downwind on a 45 and Tom reached over and covered the airspeed indicator. What?!? We never did that in practice! OK, I have to fly it by feel. On downwind, I completed the pre-landing checklist and made the appropriate radio calls. Carb heat on, reduce power for descent, 10 degrees flaps, radio call, turn to base. I was low. I added power to get back on track, then reduced power. Tom said, "Let's make this a soft field landing". OK. I stabilized and added a little power during the flare. I touched down slightly right of center with the nose wheel in the air. I rolled out a few feet and then let out the power and let the nosewheel come down. Tom asked me to keep the taxi speed up since there was someone coming in behind us. I cleared the runway, reset the flaps and carb heat, turned off the strobe lights, landing light and the transponder. I hesitated, not knowing if we were done or not. It was 9:46 A.M. After a pause, Tom finally said, "That's all, we're done." I let out a big sigh of relief!

Tom asked, "Well, how do you think you did?" I told him not very good about not finding the Wadsworth airport but good about the rest. Then he said, "Congratulations, you passed!" and he shook my hand. He told me that he was going to ask me to take him back if I hadn't found the Wadsworth airport on the last circle around. That would have meant failure. What a close call! I asked him for feedback and he said he'd give me some after I had received my ticket. That way I'd feel better about it.

YEEESSS! I did it!

I taxied to the pumps which Unicom told me were now working. Tom got out and said that he would meet me in the trailer. After fueling, the line crew towed the airplane to the hangar for me. I had walked down and opened the hangar door and we pushed the aircraft in. I logged the time (1.5 hours), and closed up the hangar. I met Tom at the trailer.

Tom asked to see my log book, written test score results and discontinuance letter. Uh-oh, I didn't have my written test score sheet with me. I thought that since he had checked it last week I didn't need it again. "No problem," he said "just go get it and I'll finish up the paperwork." He asked me to review the temporary certificate and validate the information. It looked real good! I told him I would be back in 10 minutes with my test results, and I drove home.

When I returned, Tom had finished up the paperwork, handed me the certificate and shook my hand. He said, "Now I'll give you feedback." He said, "Remember when you announced to Wadsworth that you were 4 miles northeast of the field?"

I nodded.

"Let me see your chart." He pointed to the airport and said, "You were right on top of the airport!"

What?!?!

He said, "You made a common mistake, by holding the map right side up instead of holding it in the direction that you were flying!"

I felt like an idiot!

He said, "I wanted to tell you this after you got your ticket, so you wouldn't think you didn't deserve it! I knew you'd get a good chuckle out of this!"

How embarrassing!

He said that my cross country work was excellent. My air work was very good and the only blemish was just about missing the airport that I was diverted to. I said I felt well prepared and he agreed that I must have received good instruction. He reminded me to use all available resources like the VOR, LORAN, etc. to determine my location.

We chatted about who my first passenger would be. He suggested it be Charlotte, my wife, since she had to put up with me during my training. The temporary certificate (good for 120 days) meant that I was a private pilot with full privileges. I would receive my official one in about 10 weeks. Tom congratulated me again, we shook hands and that was it.

I DID IT!

I went down and paid the bill for the airplane and left with a big, proud smile on my face, a little embarrassed about missing the airport, and the relief of knowing that it was over and I had been successful. Whew!

The final numbers were:
Total flight time 66.4 hours.
204 landings.
63 Flights.
First Lesson: 9/21/97
Checkride: 5/22/98
8 Months duration
13.1 Solo hours

EPILOGUE

It's hard to describe the sense of accomplishment that came over me when I passed the checkride. I realized that I had really just taken the first steps in learning to fly. They call it the 'license to learn' for good reason. My intent is to fly often during the summer and get more comfortable in the pilot's seat. In the fall, I think I'll start working on the instrument rating.

After I got my ticket, I flew a few times by myself before I was confident enough to take a passenger. My 13 year old son, Greg, was anxious to fly and I was just as anxious to take him. I was nervous about this trip because of the precious cargo I would carry and I wanted his first trip with Dad to be perfect.

I planned a short trip to Ashtabula, Ohio and we headed out one evening. I carefully briefed my young passenger and we departed from Kent State. We climbed up to 3500 feet and I began to relax a little bit. We took in the sights and had a marvelous trip.

I executed a near perfect landing in Ashtabula that would have impressed anyone. We taxied back to the beginning of the runway while a couple of blue herons watched. I think they had smiles on their beaks. Probably marveling at that landing.

We took off and climbed back to cruising altitude. Off in the distance, about 20 miles or so was a sight that I'll never forget. The sun was starting to dip down in the west. The brilliant, orange glow of the sun reflected off the water of Lake Erie and provided a spectacular backdrop for the skyline of Cleveland. It was outstanding! Sharing this experience with my son was truly awesome.

I know that my Dad was with us too.
That is why I learned to fly!

GLOSSARY

AGL—Above Ground Level

Aileron—The ailerons are located on the trailing edge of each wing near the wing tips. When the yoke is turned left, the left aileron goes up and the right aileron goes down. This changes the 'shape' of the wing creating more lift on the right side and less lift on the left. This causes the airplane to bank.

AIM—Aeronautical Information Manual. These are not regulations but rather accepted practices.

Airspace—sections of air above the surface classified by the FAA. Each class has specific rules and restrictions.

Airspeed Indicator—like a speedometer. It measures speed of the airplane in relation to the relative wind, not groundspeed.

Altitude—height usually measured from sea level (MSL—mean sea level), but sometimes measured from ground level (AGL—above ground level).

AME—Aviation Medical Examiner

AOPA—Aircraft Owner's and Pilot's Association. A general aviation industry group that provides it's members with aviation services.

ATC—Air Traffic Control

ATIS—Automatic Terminal Information Service. A radio broadcast around larger airports giving current winds, clouds, visibility, temperature, dewpoint, barometric pressure and active runway information.

Attitude—see pitch attitude

Carburetor heat—pulling a lever in the cockpit will redirect heated air around the carburetor to melt or inhibit ice buildup in the carburetor.

Clearing Turns—Turns made in flight, prior to maneuvers, to ensure that the area is clear of other air traffic.

Cowling—the 'hood' of the airplane covering the engine.

Crab—flying cockeyed to the direction of travel. Required to fly a straight path over the ground while compensating for wind.

Density Altitude—Pressure altitude adjusted for non- standard temperature. When the weather is hot and humid, the airplane does not perform as well as when it is cold and dry. Density altitude can be calculated so that aircraft performance can be more accurately estimated.

Directional Gyro (DG)—a gyroscopic instrument that shows direction. The gyro causes this instrument to be more stable than the magnetic compass and is therefore easier to read. The directional gyro is aligned with the magnetic compass before takeoff and may need to be adjusted during flight.

DUATS—a free computer dial-up weather service providing up-to-date aviation weather information such as current weather conditions at various airports, forecasts, weather maps, winds aloft and other use-ful weather information.

Dutch Roll—a maneuver flown by turning the yoke in one direction and using opposite rudder to maintain a straight course with one wing low. A useful maneuver during crosswind landings.

Elevator—a horizontal flipper at the tail section controlled by for-ward or backward pressure on the control yoke. It is used to control the pitch attitude of the airplane in flight.

FAA—Federal Aviation Administration

FAR—Federal Aviation Regulations.

FBO—Fixed Based Operator. Company located at an airport that provides fuel and other services.

Flaps—a flap is located on the trailing edge of each wing near the body of the airplane. Flaps change the shape of the wing to allow more drag and consequently slower controlled flight. Controlled by a mechanical lever or an electric switch in the cockpit.

Flare—Near the end of the landing approach, the pilot will slow the descent by increasing back elevator pressure, or flare, to allow for light touchdown.

Foggles—special glasses that are frosted along the top and sides so that the student can only see the instrument panel and cannot see out the windows. Used in basic instrument training.

Go-around—an aborted landing approach used whenever the pilot is not comfortable that he can make a safe landing. Could become necessary due to an obstruction on the runway, unexpected wind gusts, too high or too fast on the approach, etc.

Hobbs—a meter indicating time, similar to that used in a taxi cab. This is used for billing purposes.

IFR—Instrument Flight Rules. Navigation by instruments and traffic separation by Air Traffic Control using radar. Private pilots must acquire additional training and an instrument rating to be qualified for IFR flight.

Knots—see nautical mile.

LORAN—Long Range Navigation Radio. A radio used in navigation.

Magneto—a device that provides electrical energy to the spark plug to ignite the fuel in each cylinder to make the engine run.

Master Switch—A switch in the cockpit that turns on and off electricity from the battery or alternator. Must be on to operate any electrical device like radios or lights, but is not required to keep an airplane flying.

Medical Certificate—Class I, II or III certificate issued by an AME. A private pilot is required to have at least a current class III medical.

MSL—Mean sea level. Measurement in feet of altitude relative to sea level.

N2497Y—the tail number of a 1963 Cessna 172D. Pronounced 'November two four niner seven yankee' or 'Niner seven yankee' for short.

N54064—the tail number of a 1981 Cessna 172P. Pronounced 'November five four zero six four' or 'zero six four' for short.

N62953—the tail number of a 1981 Cessna 172P. Pronounced 'November six two niner five three' or 'niner five three' for short.

Nautical Mile—a measure of distance. A knot or nautical mile is 1.15 times the length of a statute mile. Most aeronautical distances are in reference to the nautical mile. Abbreviated NM.

Non-towered—an airport with no control tower and controller orchestrating the arrival and departure of aircraft.

Phase check—a periodic review performed by a different instructor to determine the progress made by a flight student.

Pitch attitude—the nose up or nose down position of the airplane.

PTS—Practical Test Standard. Clearly explains the knowledge and skills that must be demonstrated to an examiner during the oral and flight portions of the practical test.

Rectangular Course—a maneuver flown around a rectangle such as a field. The object is to remain an equal distance from all sides correcting for wind.

Rudder—a vertical flap attached to the tail, controlled by the foot pedals. The rudder keeps the tail following directly behind the nose of the airplane resulting in efficient and coordinated flight.

Runup—a preflight test of the magnetos. This is done by holding the brakes and revving up the engine to a defined rpm level. Once at the appropriate level, switch the key to the left magneto and note the rpm drop. Next, return the key to both for a couple of seconds and then switch the key to the right magneto and note the rpm drop. Each airplane has limits on rpm drop allowable and the maximum difference between the two magnetos.

Sectional—an aeronautical map of a section of the United States. This map shows landmarks such as cities, towns, roads, railroads, restricted areas, towers and obstructions and, of course, airports.

Short Field—a type of takeoff and landing where takeoff and landing are done in the minimum runway distance.

Slip—A maneuver where the airplane is turned one way and significant opposite rudder is applied making the airplane fly angled to one side. This presents the side of the airplane to the relative wind creating more drag and allowing for a steeper descent without significant increase in airspeed.

Slow flight—a maneuver where the airplane is flown at just above the stall speed.

Soft Field—a type of takeoff and landing where snow, grass or mud exists on the runway causing the runway to be soft.

Solo—Oh, what a feeling. One person in a flying airplane.

Stall—a stall occurs when the air is no longer flowing smoothly over and under the wing. This can occur at any speed. When a stall occurs, the nose of the airplane drops. Decreasing the angle of attack will recover from a stall.

Steep Turns—a maneuver where the pilot flies a complete circle with a 45 degree bank angle without gaining or losing altitude.

S-Turns—a maneuver where an S pattern is flown over a straight line, such as a road, maintaining the same radius of each half circle, correcting for wind.

Towered—an airport with a control tower and controller orchestrating the arrival and departure of aircraft.

Transponder—a radio that identifies an aircraft on the radar screen. Mode C transponders also report altitude to the radar controller.

Trim—a controllable flap located on the elevator, usually on one side of the tail only. Controlled by a small wheel in the cockpit. It's purpose is to relieve control yoke pressure.

TRSA—Terminal Radar Service Area. A special area of airspace controlled by radar that is not classified as class B or C airspace.

Turns around a point—a maneuver where the pilot flies a perfect circle around an obstruction on the ground such as a tree or water tower. Requires adjustment in bank angle to correct for wind conditions.

Unusual Attitude—The instructor maneuvers the airplane while the student has his head down and eyes closed. The student quickly loses track of up, down, left and right. At the appropriate time, the instructor turns the controls over to the student for recovery from the 'unusual attitude'.

VFR—Visual Flight Rules. Navigation by ground reference and traffic separation by sight. Non-instrument rated pilots may operate only in VFR conditions.

VOR—VHF Omnidirectional Radio. A radio beacon that is used for navigation.